University of Birmingham

Centre for Urban

and

Regional Studies

Studies in Sociology

Edited by

PROFESSOR W. M. WILLIAMS

University College, Swansea

3

DEMOGRAPHIC ANALYSIS

STUDIES IN SOCIOLOGY

Edited by Professor W. M. Williams

published

1 The Sociology of Industry
  by S. R. Parker, R. K. Brown, J. Child and M. A. Smith

2 Urban Sociology
  by Professor R. N. Morris

in preparation

Sociology of the Family
  by C. C. Harris

Social Stratification
  by James Littlejohn

Social Statistics
  by Bleddyn Davies

Community Studies
  by Professor W. M. Williams

The Sociology of Religion
  by M. A. Smith and P. J. Griffiths

Political Sociology
  by Philip Abrams

DEMOGRAPHIC ANALYSIS

B. Benjamin B.Sc., Ph.D., F.I.A.

Director of Research and Intelligence, Greater London Council
Formerly Director of Statistics, Ministry of Health
Author of 'Health and Vital Statistics'

London
GEORGE ALLEN AND UNWIN LTD
RUSKIN HOUSE · MUSEUM STREET

FOREWORD

THIS book is addressed to all those engaged in social studies who are not specialist demographers but nevertheless share a common need to understand population movements, which are so often the determinants of social change. For a proper understanding of population changes and their interrelationship with changes in social attitudes, some rudimentary knowledge of demographic methods is essential. This knowledge is not mathematically demanding. Most processes involve only simple arithmetic, not however without logic and not without a thorough understanding of the materials brought into the calculations. In demography as in any other field of applied statistics, the processes of classification and comparison are fundamental. Concepts and definitions are therefore important.

After an introduction to some of the tools commonly employed by demographers and to the principal sources of population data, the main text begins with the scope, content and use of the population census, the primary source of information about the population of the country and the point of departure both for intercensal estimates and for future projections.

Population change is the net effect of births, deaths and migration and separate chapters (5–8) have been devoted to methods of measuring these elements. The chapter on fertility is followed by a chapter on marriage, because the two elements are so closely interlinked. Having then determined the various contributions to population change we can put them together, estimating past or future changes. The methodology is set out in Chapter 9.

An account of demographic methods would be incomplete without a reference to sickness measurement. This is partly because sickness *is* a population characteristic and partly because an examination of disease prevalence and the factors affecting it leads to a better understanding of mortality variation.

Demographic methods are now much more used in the field of economics than formerly. The time has passed when economists could assume a population slowly increasing in size, but otherwise not significantly changing its structure. Population changes tend to be more irregular and to involve sharp alterations in structure. The implications for consumer demand and manpower supply form part of a proper understanding of the economy of the country. In addition, much more attention is now paid within industries and within establishments to career structures. To meet the needs of economists and personnel officers working in these fields a final chapter on manpower has been added.

This is a very short manual of methods with little illustrative material. For those who wish to pursue their studies beyond the bare essentials, appropriate additional references are listed at the end of each chapter.

CONTENTS

FOREWORD   vii

1   The Use of Demographic Statistics   1

2   The Tools of Demography   9

3   Source Materials   16

4   The Population Census   21

5   Fertility Measurement   53

6   Marriage Rates   67

7   Mortality Measurement   74

8   Migration   107

9   Population Estimation and Projection   112

10   Sickness Measurement   123

11   Manpower Statistics   142

INDEX   159

1

The use of demographic statistics

The total population of England and Wales at the middle of 1961 was estimated to be 46·3 millions and at the middle of 1966 it was estimated to be 48·1 millions. Over the period 1958 to 1964 it increased at the average rate of 0·8 per cent each year. Against the background of estimated annual increases (in the same period) of 2·7 per cent in Latin America, 2·2 per cent in Oceania (Australia, New Zealand, Melanesia, Polynesia, etc.), 2·3 per cent in Africa, 1·8 per cent in Asia, 1·6 per cent in North America and in USSR, and an annual increase of 1·7 per cent (an addition of 153,000 each day) to a world population total, which at mid-1965 was estimated to be 3,285 million (United Nations Demographic Yearbook 1965), the population growth of England and Wales may appear to be relatively slow. Conditions are certainly far different from some areas of Asia or Africa where high rates of population growth tend to make heavy demands on resources needed for the economic development of those areas, and frustrate efforts to raise the level of living of the people. Nevertheless, even though there is at present no problem of population pressure of these dimensions in this country there are still a number of important problems which provoke interest in current and prospective population changes.

The present rate of growth could provoke economic and social problems of some magnitude. If the present trend continues, the official projection based on mid-1966 indicates that the population of England and Wales at the end of this century will amount to 64 million. The density of population in terms of the number of persons per unit area in England and Wales is already high. The number of persons per square kilometre of area (including inland water) in 1964 in England and Wales was 314 (United Nations, 1966). In Europe the only country with more than one million inhabitants to have a higher figure was Netherlands with 361, though

came close with 307. The figure for France was only 88 and
en 17. For Europe as a whole the density was 89 persons
e kilometre: the densities in other regions of the world were
er; figures are Asia 65, Northern America 10, Latin America
12, Africa 10, Oceania 2, USSR 10, and the world as a whole 24.
In these comparisons uninhabited polar regions and some other
uninhabited areas are excluded, but there are differences in the
quality of land, for example, forest or desert areas, which mean
that comparisons are only a guide to relative density of population.
It is clear, however, that we already live so close together in this
country that any substantial increase in population will involve
pressure on accommodation, communications and services, and
encroachment on cultivable land and open spaces to an extent that
would be less bearable than in some other countries with more
elbow room. Present indications are that the increase *will* be
substantial.

In the long term, in so far as the present period of relatively slow
population growth follows an era of rapid expansion when increasing
numbers of births maintained a youthful age structure, the population
must undergo a process of ageing, that is to say older people have
been becoming and are going to become more numerous. This is
presenting problems of housing, dependency, and social welfare
of considerable magnitude. In so far as any adaptation of the
national economy will be a necessary concomitant of this ageing
process it is important for the pace of this change to be measured.

Even if population should eventually become comparatively stable
this stability may mask important changes acting in opposing direc-
tions in different sections of the population. In the past the families
of manual workers have generally been larger than those of non-
manual workers. There are also geographical and religious differentials. The extent of such differentials and the possibility of any
change in their extent is of interest to the Government in formulation
of both social and fiscal policy, and to industry and commerce in
the assessment of the home market for goods and services. In the
long term too it is likely that this country, in common with other
countries of advanced economic development, will achieve fertility
control, i.e. the gap between desired and attained family size will,
over the whole population, be narrowed to a point of small significance. This means that economic and social factors affecting fertility
will have a more direct and perhaps a more immediate effect on
population growth. Clearly for forecasting purposes more must be
learned about both the pace of approach to this situation and the
factors which will then determine fertility changes.

The Royal Commission on Population reporting in 1949 (when the annual rate of growth was only 0·3 per cent), balanced the increased density of a growing population against the advantages, viz. an increase in the scale of production with its stimulus to technical improvement, the younger age structure of population accompanying high birth rates, flexibility of labour resources without unemployment by virtue of the large intake into industry which could be attracted to points of higher demand or to new occupations, and an increase in the international influence and general economic strength of the country. They concluded that 'for the present it can be said that the uncertainties of the future regarding world suppliers of food and the opportunities for British export trade give us good reason to be thankful that no further large increases in our population are probable'. The considerations which enabled them to reach this conclusion also led them to urge the need for 'a continuous watch over population movements and their bearing on national policies'. The fact that the rate of growth has increased so dramatically since their appraisal underlines the need for this 'continuous watch'.

There is a further problem to which the Royal Commission on Population devoted some attention, namely, the need to be able to spare and indeed to encourage a sufficient flow of emigrants to sustain the British element in the Commonwealth. More recently a new problem has been created by the selective character of this migration and the possibility that Britain might be exporting higher degrees of skilled labour than are being imported. Some concern had been expressed that no statistics exist to give an accurate picture of the losses of key men whose departure may effect the economy of the country out of all proportion to their numbers. As a result some action has been taken to improve the availability of statistics of migration (see p. 109).

It was the official view in the early 1950s that though we and the Commonwealth countries would like at least half their immigrants to be of British stock, the attempt to fill this need should be regulated by the state of our own economy, and should take account of the relative skills of the migrants (to the United Kingdom) by whom they are replaced. It was further thought that in order to maintain the supply of emigrants in the longer term future without detriment to the youthfulness of the population of this country, some increase in the birth rate would be desirable. In fact an increase did take place from 1955 and persisted until 1965.

Regardless of any of these problems, knowledge of population changes is essential to Government Departments, to Local Authorities and to planning organizations in order to estimate national and local needs in education, employment, health services, housing, social security and defence.

As a result of large fluctuations in the birth rate, the number of children in England and Wales in the primary and secondary school age groups have varied, and will vary, considerably as can be seen from Table One.

TABLE ONE

Numbers of children of school
age in England and Wales 1938–86
(thousands)

Mid-year	Age	
	5–10	11–15
1946	3,386	2,790
1951	3,740	2,822
1956	4,267	3,052
1961	3,911	3,675
1966	4,292	3,265
Forecast:[1]		
1971	4,931	3,515
1976	5,073	4,103
1981	5,433	4,197
1986	5,651	4,512

[1] The forecast figures are based on the population projection prepared by the Government Actuary's Department in consultation with the General Register Office, and published in the Quarterly Return for the quarter ended December 31, 1966. (A more recent projection may have appeared before the present text is published but it is the trend rather than the precise forecast values in Table One which is important.)

The education authorities have thus had to face a great expansion in accommodation needs, first for primary schools and later for secondary schools. Such an expansion has made very large demands on capital investment both in material terms of new school building and equipment and in human terms of training additional teachers. There has been a geographical differential in this demand, the pressure being greater in those areas of housing development where resources are also most strained to produce new services of many kinds. Moreover, if a rise in the birth rate is temporary, then ten years after it has exhausted itself the new school accommodation will not be so much in demand for primary education and fifteen years later the pressure for secondary education accommodation will be lessened. There has therefore had to be careful planning to strike a balance between building and making do with existing accommodation (with the additional restraint of limited capital resources) in order to ensure that there is not too much permanent building for temporary need. Here the provision of adequate population statistics is an essential prerequisite. The prospects for the supply of manpower in the future are determined by the trend of births. This indicates the size of generations expected to enter the working age period in later years. The information is qualified by facts derived from the periodical population census concerning the number of persons currently employed in different industries and different occupations at different ages. Such facts as these indicate the likely changes in the age structure of those employed in particular occupations and industries and indicate current experience with regard to ages of recruitment and of retirement. Further light on recruitment and skill distribution is shed by the census information about duration of education of persons in different occupations. More recently this has been supplemented by studies of the work content (i.e. the skills and training required) of particular occupations. This is all in the nature of basic information for long term planning. Short periods statistics of employment are derived by the Government from returns from employers of numbers employed and from returns from labour exchanges of numbers unemployed; indicators of trend are provided by the statistics of unfilled vacancies and of vacancies notified to exchanges.

With regard to health services, it is necessary to know not only what diseases to prevent but also where these diseases are especially likely to occur. Those responsible for the organization of the services have to assess certain risks, their present values and trends, which are often specific to a particular section of the population. The particular attribute which renders a certain group within the general population more or less susceptible to a disease may be one of many—age, sex, birthplace, occupation, urbanization, geographical region, and other environmental and social factors. Cases of disease occurring in these segments of the population have to be related to numbers at risk. These numbers are only known precisely at the time of the population census; at intermediate dates, estimates have to be based upon such information of post-censal movement as may be available from vital registration, returns to Government Departments and other sources.

Artistic and amenity considerations aside, any planned development of urban areas and the housing of over-crowded areas, must take into account the relationship between the existing stock of dwellings and the prospective distribution of households by size and contribution. For example, at the 1951 Census, it was possible to compare the existing distribution of household occupations by numbers of rooms with the distribution which would be required to certain hypothetical room allocations, allowing in particular for the separation of potentially distinct households ('family nuclei') from the composite households containing them (a common example would be a married son and his wife living with his parents). The following table is reproduced from the Housing Report (General Register Office, 1956) as an illustration.

TABLE TWO

Great Britain—Size of household occupations, compared with hypothetical room allocations, to allow for family nuclei to be housed separately

| Number of Rooms | Hypothetical household occupations (hundreds) allowing habitable rooms per household in addition to bedrooms as follows: | | | | Actual household occupations (hundreds) |
| | Two for each household or family nucleus | One for each household of one person; two for each larger household or family nucleus | One for each household of one person and for one half of the larger household or family nuclei, two for the remainder | One for each household | |
(1)	(2)	(3)	(4)	(5)	(6)
1					470,1
2		1,906,2	3,691,5	5,476,9	1,447,7
3	5,476,9¹	3,570,7	5,040,1	6,509,5	2,355,7
4	6,509,5	6,509,5	4,590,8	2,672,1	3,849,2
5	2,672,1	2,672,1	1,660,3	648,4	4,242,3
6	648,4	648,4	385,1	121,9	1,375,3
7 or more	156,8	156,8	95,9	34,9	741,2
Total households	15,463,7	15,463,7	15,463,7	15,463,7	14,481,5

¹ The insertion of the comma after the first digit of each figure is intended to remind readers that results were based on a one per cent sample.

The comment was made that 'if it is justifiable to think that most opinions about housing adequacy lie somewhere between the extremes (cols. (2) and (5)) it would appear that in 1951 there were too few two- and three-room units of accommodation for one- and two-person households, particularly when it is remembered that the very great majority of these small households are composed of middle-aged and elderly persons, and few comprise married couples whose family building is in front of them . . .'

Another aspect of population measurement closely related to the planning of housing development, is that of internal migration. It would be useless to pursue long term building projects in areas from which economic or other influences have compelled the population to drift away. Equally some account has to be taken of the fact that in areas with apparently stationary populations large self-balancing movements may be constantly occurring and producing changes in the internal structure of the community.

With regard to social security it is sufficient only to refer to the size of the annual Exchequer outgo now represented by the National Insurance schemes—some £5,700 million,[1] and note that this is the emergence of a contracted liability which will emerge relentlessly as annual charges upon the Exchequer to the extent that it is not offset by contributions from insured persons and employers or interest on funds. It is essential therefore that the rate of emergence of liabilities, and the strain on the economy, must be forecast with reasonable accuracy in order that the necessary fiscal action can be taken in good time.

Estimating the increase of pensions costs and other social insurance benefits is a matter of population projection. In his Report on the first Quinquennial Review of the Operation of the National Insurance Act 1946 the Government Actuary considered it necessary to devote a full Appendix to the discussion of the estimates of the future population of Great Britain upon which his financial forecasts were based.

Finally, on the subject of defence, it is obvious that the manpower needs of the defence services and the scale of the commitments that can be safely assumed must be balanced against estimates of populations changes, especially of the availability of young adults in the future, and of any competitive demands of industry.

So far we have considered only the governmental needs for population statistics. There are many other interests. In industry, especially on the distributive side, modern methods of market research involve the widespread use of sample survey techniques. As a basis for stratification and for sampling control, up-to-date and soundly based population statistics are essential. The growth of urban populations, especially where this involves greater dispersal from workplaces, is the constant concern of transport undertakings.

[1] See *Report on the Third Quinquennial Review of the Operation of the National Insurance Acts 1946–64.*

Everyone with something to sell or a service to offer is interested in the number of potential users. Even the man in the street takes stock of his neighbours and, either because he seeks the 'madding crowd' or seeks to avoid it, gives some thought consciously or subconsciously to their numbers.

This manual is an account of modern practice in population measurement, but discussion is not restricted to those methods or forms of presentation which are actually employed in official publications. The opportunity has been taken to place on record ideas that have occurred in the development of current methods, and which though not necessarily of practical consequence in themselves may stimulate more fruitful discussion.

REFERENCES

Demographic Yearbook 1965. Statistical Office, U.N. Department of Economic and Social Affairs (1966). (This yearbook is issued annually and usually features a particular topic, e.g. fertility; it is a standard reference on world demography.)

Report of the Royal Commission on Population, Cmd. 7695 H.M.S.O (1949).

Government Actuary: *Report on the Third Quinquennial Review of the Operation of the National Insurance Acts 1946–64.* H.M.S.O. (1964).

Housing Report, Census 1951. General Register Office (1956).

2

The tools of demography

It will be useful to take a quick look round the demographer's workshop before commencing a detailed review of methods. The student can then see what range of knowledge he must encompass and the situations which he is likely to meet.

The demographer is concerned with measuring past, and forecasting future, population change. To do so he must isolate and quantify not only the principal elements of fertility, mortality and migration but also the underlying factors concerned in these elements, for example the social and economic influences at work.

As in any technology, care has to be taken to *define* the *concepts* used and the measures by reference to which they are described. This is essential for comparability and communication. If reference is made to a population group, for example, married women or non-manual supervisors or school leavers, then the content of that group must be clearly and unequivocally defined. This is particularly important where, for example, rates of mortality are being calculated. If in assigning individuals to a particular group those who die are treated differently from those who survive, the death rates will be distorted. In referring to the population of a country it would be necessary to indicate whether this referred to people actually *in* the country at a point of time, i.e. including visitors from overseas but excluding those normally in the country but temporarily abroad; or whether it referred, for example, to all those claiming the country's nationality whatever their current location; and whether there was any restriction applying, for example, to non-civilians.

RELATIVE MEASURES

The frequency of occurrence of *characteristics* in the population will normally be measured in *proportions*. Actual numbers are usually meaningless unless related to the size of the population under examination. To say that there are 5·83 million persons of age sixty-five and over in England and Wales and 0·58 million in Scotland

9

tells us nothing about the age structures of the two countries. When these numbers are expressed as proportions of the total population of each country, 12·2 and 11·1 per cent respectively, we not only get a better mental picture (one in eight) of the frequency of this age group in the population of England and Wales but we can compare the frequency in two countries of widely differing size of population.

Relative measures (i.e. relative to the population) are also necessary to describe the frequency of occurrence of events. Common examples are births, marriages, entry in institutions, retirements from employment, deaths. Other forms of relative measure occur in respect of characteristics such as housing occupancy (rooms) which have to be related to population (persons). Such a ratio (persons per room) may be specific to a particular household size (households of x persons). There are other density measures such as persons per acre or dwellings per acre or retail shopping floor space per unit population.

Single Figure Indices

Mortality and fertility vary with age and many other factors. In order to be able to compare like with like it is therefore necessary to have regard to sets of rates specific for these factors. A whole page of specific rates is difficult to assimilate mentally and there is always a demand for a single figure index that might summarize a large number of specific rates. Invariably such a single figure is a *weighted average* or aggregate of the rates which it is claimed to represent. For example, there is the age standardized rate of mortality —an average of the age specific rates in which each age group rate is weighted by the number, in the particular age group, in some standard population. There is the gross reproduction rate in which age specific fertility rates for women are weighted by the number of women in each age group in a stable population generated by a constant number of female births. The interpretation and use of the index depends upon the weights used and no such index should be used without careful examination of its content.

The Life Table

One way of illustrating the significance of a set of mortality rates (an early example of a 'model') is to follow a generation of births from age to age throughout life, subjecting them to these rates of mortality at successive ages and observing their survival. A convenient number of births, say 100,000 (termed the radix of the table), is taken and interest lies in seeing how many survive to age 10, 20, 30, etc., in comparison with a table based on different mortality rates.

Other useful parameters such as the average length of life (expectation of life) may be derived from the table.
The following abridged form of table is a typical specimen.

TABLE THREE

Abridged life table, 1952, England and Wales

Age x	Males Survivors l_x	Males Deaths d_x	Females Survivors l_x	Females Deaths d_x
0	10,000	309	10,000	241
1	9,691	22	9,759	18
2	9,669	13	9,741	10
3	9,656	10	9,731	7
4	9,646	7	9,724	6
5	9,639	28	9,718	20
10	9,611	24	9,698	17
15	9,587	43	9,681	25
20	9,544	64	9,656	37
25	9,480	61	9,619	47
30	9,419	74	9,572	57
35	9,345	102	9,515	78
40	9,243	149	9,437	118
45	9,094	257	9,319	179
50	8,837	447	9,140	272
55	8,390	699	8,868	402
60	7,691	988	8,466	606
65	6,703	1,313	7,860	916
70	5,390	1,533	6,944	1,314
75	3,857	1,605	5,630	1,731
80	2,252	1,385	3,899	2,082
85	867	649	1,817	1,209
90	218	188	608	483
95	30	30	125	125

The notation is explained on p. 95 of Chapter 7 where the life table is dealt with fully. Suffice it to say here that l_x denotes the number surviving to exact age x and d_x is the number dying between exact age x and the next (exact) age shown in the table. Thus $d_{20} = l_{20} - l_{25}$.

The Nuptiality Table

Just as the life table is used to illustrate mortality experience, we may use a similar model to illustrate the marriage experience of men or women, more often the latter. Here we follow a generation of female births through life subjecting them to two decrements— marriage and death. We are interested not only in the number surviving at each stage, but in the proportions of those who have remained single and those who have become married.

SICKNESS MEASUREMENT

There are a number of special concepts and definitions in use for disease measurement. The Statistics Sub-Committee of the Registrar General's Advisory Committee on Medical Nomenclature and Statistics examined the problem of defining morbidity measures (1954) in two stages: (i) the choice of descriptive words, e.g. the substitution, for the general term 'sickness', of words more specific-ally describing the character of the condition measured, such as 'sickness absence', 'in-patient care', 'general practitioner consulta-tion'; the substitution of 'inception' (to indicate 'beginning') for 'incidence' which is too broad in current usage; (ii) classification and definition of rates, i.e. distinction between rates relating to inception, prevalence, duration and fatality respectively. An impor-tant recommendation is that relating to the measure which the actuary has always called a 'sickness rate'. This is called 'the average duration of sickness per person' (short title—'average duration per person') and is defined as 'The total duration within a defined period of all spells of sickness that occurred wholly or partly within that period divided by the average number of persons exposed to risk during the period'. Other rates in common use are (i) new cases of disease occurring in a period (inception rate) per unit number of persons at risk, (ii) cases of disease existing at a point of time (prevalence rate) per unit number of persons at risk, (iii) frequency rates of consultation, i.e. consultations per unit number of persons at risk. It is important that all such measures should be subjected to close scrutiny in order to ascertain whether their meaning is sufficiently explicit and is capable of precise definition, whether they are the most convenient to calculate, and whether they are most adapted to the purposes for which they are being employed.

POPULATION PROJECTION

In order to bring out the implications of current trends in mor-tality, fertility, and migration it is useful to apply these factors to the population of the country in successive years in the future, starting with the present population size and structure. Such a calculation, termed a projection, may be looked upon as a 'model' for demonstrating the ultimate effect of present trends *if continued* without necessarily implying that they *will* be continued. It should therefore be distinguished from a forecast. Commonly a number of projections are produced based upon alternative assumptions of future trends.

SAMPLING AND FIELD STUDIES

Vital registration records and other standard sources of health statistics (infectious disease notifications, hospital discharge records, cancer registration systems, etc.) may from time to time require to be supplemented by specially organized studies involving direct observation of disease incidence or of social and economic characteristics in the population.

Often, on the grounds of cost, such observation has to be limited to a sample of the population. Such economy of effort is possible since well developed techniques are available to ensure that the sample is truly representative of the population and likely to yield reliable estimates of the factors to be measured.

The advantage of sampling (as compared with a total survey) lies primarily in the fact that for a sufficient amount of information smaller resources are required; or, what is often more important, for the same resources more information can be sought under time-consuming but more rewarding conditions of contact and general supervision. Families are mobile and are not always where you expect to find them and even if the interviewees for a particular survey are resident at their usual address they may be out a good deal so that several visits would be required to establish contact. It may take more than one interview or at least a very long interview to question the respondent with such a degree of carefulness and penetration as would be required to attain a desired level of accuracy. In health surveys it may be desirable to carry out medical examinations or make diagnostic tests. All these procedures are expensive in time and manpower. High quality response over a restricted (but representative) field is more useful than poor quality response from larger numbers; and in fact larger coverage may be impracticable. Limited, high-quality response will usually produce quicker results, for the processing of data takes longer than most people expect especially where complex classifications have to be made and coded.

REQUIREMENTS OF A GOOD SAMPLE

Since the ultimate object is to generalize about the total population, the sample must be so chosen as to be likely to correctly reflect the

distribution of characteristics in the total population. The sample
must cover the whole distribution in proper proportions and must
not be biased, i.e. tend to contain one part of the distribution more
than another. For example, in any survey of physical measurements
of men the sample must be likely to contain short and tall men in
the same proportions as in the general population and not be biased
in such a way as to contain more than a fair share of tall men or

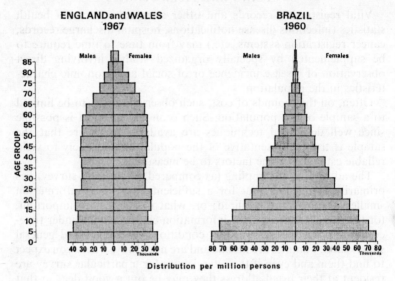

Fig. 1. Population Pyramids

short men. The words 'be likely to' are important. No system of
sampling can ensure perfect correspondence. There are bound to be
chance differences between the constitution of the sample and that
of the parent population. The possible extent of these unbiased
chance differences, or sampling errors, which will not have a tendency to be in a particular direction, can be estimated in advance
and can be reduced to any desired level by increasing the size of the
sample. Bias, if inherent in the system, will tend to be in a particular
direction and will not be reduced by increasing the size of the sample.

Bias arises when the system of selection itself or the degree of
response does not give equal likelihood to the representation of
members of the population, i.e. fails to follow a random process,
or where the rules for that process are not strictly adhered to.

THE REPRESENTATION OF AGE STRUCTURES

The population pyramid is a useful way of illustrating the age structure of population. In such a pyramid (Fig. 1) each age group is represented by a rectangle of area proportional to the number in the age group. Sometimes the absolute number in the age group is thus represented by a rectangle but more commonly, for standardization of size of diagram, the proportion (per million of total) is used. The rectangles are placed on top of each other, the youngest age group at the bottom and the oldest at the top. The height of each rectangle represents the age interval and the length for *equal* age intervals is therefore proportional to the numbers in the age groups. Care should be taken, however, if unequal age intervals have to be used, to adjust the lengths to ensure that the *areas* of the rectangles are proportional to numbers. It is usual to set the rectangles for males on one side of the diagram and those for females on the other, the origin of rectangles being from the centre of the diagram. This arrangement gives rise to the pyramid shape. A pyramid based on a national population census can indicate a great deal about population conditions in the country. A squat pyramid is typical of a country in an early stage of demographic development with a high birth rate, a high death rate, and a youthful age structure. A tall pyramid is typical of low mortality with large proportions surviving to older age groups. A pyramid which is narrow at the foot and bulges out in the middle, indicates that there has been a fall in the flow of births and that more recent generations are smaller than their predecessors.

REFERENCES

Benjamin, B. *Health and Vital Statistics*. Allen and Unwin, London (1968).
Measurement of Morbidity, Studies on Medical and Population Subjects. General Register Office (1954).
Bradford Hill, A. *Medical Statistics*, 8th edition. *Lancet*, London (1966).
Cox, P. R. *Demography*, 3rd edition. Cambridge University Press (1959).
Yates, F. *Sampling Methods for Censuses and Surveys*, 2nd edition. C. Griffin and Co. Ltd., London (1953).

Source materials

THE measurements of population, from the analysis of which the demographer seeks to draw conclusions about structure, change and the determinants of change, have to be obtained from a count of *heads* or a count of *events*. The count of heads, i.e. the population census, is a basic source of data and the whole of the next chapter has been devoted to it. The events to be counted are births, deaths, marriages and migrations. The first three are subject to compulsory registration, the last is not. Reference should be made to the chapter on migration for methods of estimating the number of these events.

BIRTHS REGISTRATION

Under the Births and Deaths Registration Act 1953 it is required that the father and mother of every child born alive or in their default by death or inability 'the occupier of the house in which a child was to the knowledge of that occupier born', or 'any person present at the birth', or 'any person having charge of the child' shall give to the Registrar within forty-two days from the date of the birth information of the particulars required to be registered. These particulars, which are separately prescribed by regulations made under the Act, are:

(*a*) Date and place of birth
(*b*) Name, if any
(*c*) Sex
(*d*) Name and surname of father
(*e*) Name and maiden surname of mother
(*f*) Father's occupation
(*g*) Signature, description and residence of informant.

An Act of 1926 had instituted the compulsory registration of still-births (over twenty-eight weeks gestation) and this is consolidated in the 1953 Act. Similar information is recorded as for live births and, in addition, there is a record of the nature of the evidence showing the child to have been stillborn which must be either a certificate signed by a medical practitioner or midwife that the child was not born alive, or a declaration by the informant in a prescribed form that no medical practitioner or midwife has attended or examined the baby, or that no certificate can be obtained and that the child was not born alive. The cause of stillbirth, as given on the doctor's or midwife's certificate, has been recorded since 1960 under the Population (Statistics) Act, 1960. Under the Population (Statistics) Act 1960 additional information may be sought upon registration; these additional details are for statistical purposes only, are therefore treated as confidential and are not entered in any public register. The details are:

On registration of live birth or stillbirth
(a) Age of mother
(b) Where the name of any person is to be entered in the register as father of the child, the age of that person
(c) Except where the birth is of an illegitimate child—

    (i) the date of the parent's marriage
    (ii) whether the mother had been married before her marriage to the father of the child
    (iii) the number of children of the mother by her present husband and by any former husband, and how many of them were born alive or were stillborn.

NOTIFICATION UNDER THE PUBLIC HEALTH ACTS

In England, apart from registration, it is required by the Public Health Act 1936 that the person in attendance on the birth, and the parent if residing at the place of birth, shall notify the local health authority (County or County Borough Council) within thirty-six hours in order that Health Visitors may make early visits for welfare purposes. This applies equally to live births or stillbirths. It is customary for local registrars and local health officers to compare their lists of registrations and notifications and the reciprocal reporting of discrepancies over a period of time in order to allow for the lag between notification and registration, leads to a high degree of accuracy in records.

The details furnished on birth notification (by postcard to the local health authority) include name, address, date and place of birth, whether live or stillborn, and birth weight.

CORRECTION FOR RESIDENCE

In England, while births are required to be registered in the area of *occurrence*, they are reallocated by the General Register Office for statistical purposes to the area of *residence* of the mother. This prevents a local birth rate from being inflated by the presence of large maternity hospitals. Local health authorities similarly transfer notifications of non-resident births.

REGISTRATION OF DEATHS

Every medical practitioner attending the deceased in his last illness is required to furnish a certificate 'stating the cause of death to the best of his knowledge and belief' and to deliver it forthwith to the Registrar. The Registrar cannot give a certificate authorizing the disposal of the body until this has been done and he is satisfied that, if the case is one which should be reported to the Coroner, the Coroner has completed his investigations. Unless the Coroner holds an inquest, information for the registration of every death has to be delivered to the Registrar of the district within five days of its occurrence by any relative of the deceased present at the death or in attendance at the last illness; or failing these by any other relative of the deceased dwelling or being in the same district as the deceased; or such person present at the death; or the occupier of the house or any inmate of the house; or the person causing the body of the deceased to be buried. If the deceased did not die in a house a comparable chain of responsibility is followed. If within the five days a qualified informant sends written notice of the death to the registrar together with a doctor's notice of signing the medical certificate of cause of death, the period for full registration is extended to fourteen days.

The cause of death is entered in the register from the medical or Coroner's certificate but in the very rare cases where there is no such certificate it is entered on the best information available. In 1963, 82·6 per cent of all deaths were certified by medical practitioners and 17·2 per cent were certified as the result of inquest, or Coroner's post-mortem without inquest; 0·2 per cent were uncertified.

Deaths are reallocated to place of residence in the same way as are births.

The information required by regulation under the Births and Deaths Registration Act 1953 to be registered for deaths is as follows:

(*a*) Date and place of death
(*b*) Name, surname
(*c*) Sex
(*d*) Age
(*e*) Occupation (in the case of women, deceased's own occupation for a spinster or divorced woman; husband's or deceased husband's occupation for a married woman or a widow)

(*f*) Cause of death
(*g*) Signature, description and residence of informant
(*h*) Date of registration
(*i*) Signature of registrar

Additional particulars recorded at death registration under the Population (Statistics) Act 1960 are:

(*a*) Whether the deceased was single, married, widowed or divorced
(*b*) The age of the surviving spouse, if any, of the deceased

Registration of Marriages

In England and Wales the information recorded at civil marriages or by the person solemnizing a religious marriage, and transmitted to the Registrar, comprises:

(*a*) Date of marriage
(*b*) Names and surnames
(*c*) Ages
(*d*) Marital conditions
(*e*) Occupations
(*f*) Residences at time of marriage
(*g*) Fathers' names and surnames
(*h*) Occupations of fathers
(*i*) The precise place of marriage
(*j*) Form of ceremony

Statistical Analyses

From these registrations, transcription records are prepared and are transmitted for data-processing by the General Register Office. The resulting tabulations appear in the weekly, quarterly and annual publications of the Registrar General. Thorough acquaintance with the contents of these publications is essential for any one seriously interested in demography. An up-dated list of contents will be found in the current edition of the General Register Office pamphlet 'Matters of Life and Death' (H.M.S.O.).

REFERENCES

Readers in Britain are advised to obtain a good working knowledge of the publications of the General Register Office of England and Wales, and the General Register Office of Scotland. Readers elsewhere should similarly acquaint themselves with the publications of their national population office. In Britain the main demographic journals are:

Population Studies (quarterly) published by the Population Investigation Committee, London.

Eugenics Review (quarterly) published by the Eugenics Society, London.

There is often a demographic content in *New Society* (weekly).

Reference should also be made to:

Milbank Memorial Quarterly, New York.

Population (quarterly) (French with English summaries) published by L'Institut National D'Etudes Demographiques, Paris.

Population Index, a quarterly bibliography issued jointly by the Office of Population Research at Princeton University, New Jersey, USA and the Population Association of America.

4

The population census

THE primary source of information about the population of a country is the population census which is taken in Britain and in most other developed countries of the world at regular intervals, usually of ten years, sometimes less. Although the population census considered as a field operation has much in common with other kinds of field survey, it is nevertheless sharply distinguished by its traditional background, legal sanctions, coverage, and by the whole scale of the operation and the resources normally devoted to it, which permit a far greater content and depth of analysis than can normally be encompassed in other types of field study.

DEFINITION OF A CENSUS

The words used internationally to describe a population census are as follows: 'A census of population may be defined as the total process of collecting, compiling, and publishing demographic, economic, and social data pertaining, at a specified time or times, to all persons in a country or delimited territory.'

Certain essential features follow from this definition. An official census is sponsored by the government of the area or of some larger region within which the area falls. The area covered is precisely defined. The principle of universality applies. The enumeration should either include every member of the community to which the census relates without omission or duplication or, if sampling is used, must give every member of a stratum equal likelihood of inclusion. For reasons which will be discussed later, it is desirable to include every member of the community in the basic enumeration and to reserve the use of sampling for the economical collection of data on supplementary topics.

LEGAL BASIS FOR THE CENSUS

Population censuses carried out in Great Britain are at present covered by the Census Act of 1920, the main provisions of which are:

21

(a) Power is given to the Registrars General of England and Wales, and Scotland, respectively, under the control and direction of the Minister of Health, to hold enumerations at intervals of not less than five years.

(b) The direction to take a census is to be by Order in Council, and may be for Great Britain or any part of Great Britain (the minimum time interval is specific to a particular part; i.e. a census cannot be 'taken in any part of Great Britain in any year unless at the commencement of that year at least five years have elapsed since the commencement of the year in which a census was last taken in that part. . . .').

(c) The questions to be asked at any census are to be prescribed by the Order in Council, but must fall within the following general scope of topics as listed in the Schedule to the 1920 Act.

  (i) Names, sex, age
  (ii) Occupation, profession, trade or employment
  (iii) Nationality, birthplace, race, language
  (iv) Place of abode, character of dwelling
  (v) Condition as to marriage, relation to head of family, issue born in marriage
  (vi) Any other matters with respect to which it is desirable to obtain statistical information with a view to ascertaining the social or civil condition of the population. (Any questions specified under this heading come under the close scrutiny of Parliament, since these must be the subject of an affirmative resolution of both Houses.)

(d) The Registrar General may at the cost of any local authority or private person satisfy a 'reasonable' request for statistical information derived from the census but not contained in the published reports. (The use of this provision has increased and is likely to increase as a result of an increased demand for data specific to a local or sectional population but not of sufficient general interest to warrant incorporation in the main tabulations of the census.)

RESTRAINTS UPON THE SCOPE OF CENSUS INQUIRIES

The scope of paragraph (f) of the Schedule to the 1920 Act is very wide, but it has to be borne in mind that two important restrictions may operate to limit the amount of information which can be made available to research workers. First, the requirement that these topics shall be the subject of affirmative resolution by both Houses of Parliament means that any topic which may offend public opinion (e.g. a question about personal incomes) or which appears to be too remotely connected with the main objective of the census as an instrument of social administration is likely to be ruled out. Secondly, Census questions which supply information essential to the business of government or directly useful to the community at large (which pays taxes to meet the bill), are likely to come before other topics, especially those related to a specialized demand and not commanding wide interest. Further, a ceiling is bound to be placed upon the total cost of the census, and since processing cost is roughly proportional to the number of questions, this number is bound to be effectively limited.

Apart from these considerations, there is a practical restriction on the extent of the census inquiries. Merely to ask an additional question in the census schedule does not ensure a correct answer. Any progressive elaboration of the schedule is likely to reach a stage at which indifference, if not resentment, will introduce inaccuracy, and this may cause doubt to be cast on the validity of the whole enumeration. This is a very important consideration where the householder is required to complete the schedule, but even where canvassers are employed, steps have to be taken to reduce the burden of questions to be directed to any one household. If the number of aspects on which population statistics are sought (additional to the basic details of age, sex, marital condition, size of household and dwelling, etc.) are too numerous to be covered at one census without excessive complexity in the schedule, it is better to cover them some at a time by a set of supplemental questions at successive censuses, especially if these by virtue of their simplicity can be held more frequently than at ten-year intervals.

Certain technical problems arise if sampling is used. If, as is more convenient, systematic rather than random sampling is adopted, steps have to be taken to avoid the bias which is often associated with the former method. In the United States census of 1950, for example, the conditions under which new enumeration sheets were completed gave rise to some degree of association between population characteristics and the order of line on the sheet. This did not seriously affect the 20-per cent sample, but it was found that for the $3\frac{1}{3}$-per cent sample, which consisted of the persons listed on the last sample line of each schedule, persons in small households were under-represented (by about 4 per cent) as a result of the instruction given to enumerators to start a new sheet whenever the set of twelve housing lines on the back of a schedule had been completed, thus leaving some lines blank on the front of the schedules where population questions were recorded. In the self-enumeration type of census (as in the United Kingdom) with a household schedule there is a choice between (i) a systematic selection of serially listed households using complementary numbers to avoid bias (as in the selection of the 1951 one per cent sample), and (ii) some system of shuffling schedules of different types before distribution. The scale of the operation militates against refined methods and some degree of departure from high standards of randomization has to be accepted.

Steps must also be taken to reduce sampling errors, for example by regression methods based on relationship of sample values to values recorded in complete enumeration and by intelligent choice of sampling fraction.

A further problem is presented by the need for cross-tabulation of several factors; this can only be effected for those members of the population who have been asked *all* of the relevant questions. This need does in fact operate as a serious restraint upon the possible sharing out of questions to ease the burden of response; for most of the answers asked for in British censuses, such as those on occupation, industry, education, require correlation one with another in tabulation and so the questions must all appear on the *same* schedule. In practice therefore sampling would be used not to increase the total questions asked but to reduce the total number of persons required to answer any questions at all other than those which are involved in the simplest exact count of heads. For such a count is required as a sure starting-point for the intercensal estimates of local populations that form the basis of Exchequer Grants, and here not only must justice be done but it must be seen to be done. The idea would be to have two schedules, one containing only questions on age, sex, marital condition, and addressed to $(100 - x)$ per cent of the population, and another containing the full battery of questions but addressed to only x per cent of the population (where x is determined by reference to the likely sampling errors in the smallest cells of the tabulation).

EARLIER CENSUSES IN GREAT BRITAIN

In England and Wales and Scotland the first census was held in 1801, and others took place at decennial intervals to 1931. World war rendered it inexpedient to have a census in 1941, and the fifteenth took place in 1951. The census of 1801 counted the number of males and females of each house and family and the number of persons engaged in agriculture, trade, manufacture, or handicraft, and other occupations not specially classified. That of 1821 was the first at which information was sought as to age, but it was left optional whether this should be furnished or not. Just prior to the 1841 census the civil registration of births, deaths, and marriages had been instituted in England and Wales and the newly appointed local Registrars replaced the parish overseers as the officers responsible for conducting the census. In addition the duty of completing the enumeration form for each family was delegated to the head of the household instead of to an official, thus enabling simultaneous entry of every person to be made. In Scotland civil registration was not established until 1855 and the census of 1841 was entrusted to the official schoolmaster or other fit person. (The Scottish census of 1861 was the first to be conducted by the Registrar-General for Scotland.) The census of 1851 was carried out under Dr William Farr's supervision and was more detailed than earlier enumerations. The questions concerned occupation, birthplace, relationship (husband, wife, etc.), marital condition (married, widowed, bachelor, etc.), education, and the number of persons deaf and dumb or blind; and, for the first time, the precise age at last birthday of each person had to be furnished.

In the census report of 1881, the age and sex distribution of the population of each urban and rural sanitary authority as then constituted was given for the first time.

At the census of 1891 the schedule contained new questions as to number of rooms and of their occupants in all tenements with less than five rooms; and an important economic distinction was made between employers, employees, and those working on their own account. In 1901 no further additions were made to the subjects of inquiry.

In 1911 a number of important changes were made. The difficulty of defining a 'house' was avoided by the enumeration for each urban and rural district of the number of various classes of buildings used as dwellings—ordinary dwelling houses, blocks of flats and the separate flats or dwellings composing them, shops, institutions, etc., with the corresponding populations. The limited accommodation inquiry of the 1891 census was extended to tenements of all sizes. The industry as well as the occupation of each worker was recorded. The tabulations gave ages in single years of life instead of groupings.

The most important development of 1911 was a detailed inquiry into fertility. The following questions were asked in respect of every married woman.

(a) Duration of marriage in completed years.
(b) The number of children born alive to the present marriage who:

(i) were still alive at the census
(ii) had died before the census.

This information was related to other census data as to age, marital status, occupation, etc., and enabled a study of area and social class differences in marriage and childbearing experience to be attempted.

In preparing for the census of 1921 it was thought that a point had been reached in progressive enlargement of census inquiries at which any further addition to the total quantity of information might lead to indifference or resistance and consequent inaccuracy. Most of the changes were therefore in the nature of substitutions. The fertility inquiry of 1911 was not repeated, on the ground that in 1921 such an inquiry would have reflected not normal experience but the disturbance of the 1914–18 war, but instead the schedule was designed to seek dependency information, i.e. details of all living children and step-children under the age of sixteen for each married man, widower, or widow on the schedule (whether these children were enumerated on the same schedule or not). Such information as to the numbers and ages of existing children according to age and marital status of parent was essential to the development of national widows' and orphans' pensions provision then contemplated. The questions as to infirmities (blind, deaf, dumb, and lunatics) of earlier censuses were dropped, since it was generally recognized that there was a natural reluctance to disclose these which militated against completeness in response; but a new question was added as to place of work. New industrial and occupational classifications were introduced.

Although as at previous censuses the 1931 enumeration was on a *de facto* basis, i.e. each person was enumerated where found at the time the census was taken instead of at the usual place of residence (referred to as the *de jure* basis), for the first time a question was inserted in the schedule asking for a statement of the address of usual residence of each person enumerated in the household. The 1931 schedule omitted any inquiry into education, workplace, and either dependency or fertility, and was thus simpler than in 1921. This reduction in scope was made partly for economy and also because it was anticipated that in future more frequent enumerations would be made and that emphasis would be placed at different times on different additions to this minimum in order to spread the complete survey over several censuses. (It was intended to hold a census in 1936, but it was later decided not to fulfil this intention.) As a reflection of the economic depression of the time the 1931 schedule was extended to include particular mention of those 'out of work'.

THE 1951 CENSUS

The enumeration was carried out as at midnight of April 8–9, 1951 in England, Wales and Scotland. In addition to the customary questions as to age, sex, marital condition, occupation, etc., special questions were included on fertility, education, household amenities (W.C., bath, etc.) and place of work.

THE 1961 CENSUS

Innovations in the 1961 enumeration included questions on tenure of dwelling, movement of usual address, and scientific qualifications; and the use of sampling in enumeration (ninety per cent of the population were asked only questions on sex, age, marital condition, birthplace, citzenship, and fertility).

THE 1966 CENSUS

The census of 1966 was conducted entirely on 10 per cent household sample basis and included new questions on the ownership and garaging of motor car, means of travel to work, and employment supplementary to main occupation.

INTERNATIONAL RECOMMENDATIONS

The Statistical Office of the United Nations have published a report on 'Principles and Recommendations for National Population Censuses' in which they submit a list of topics to be covered. The list (given below) is prefaced by the reservation 'Because of the many factors which determine the topics to be covered by any national census, no inflexible recommended list is desirable. The topics of general national and international value given below are those in most universal use which have emerged after decades of census experience as of greatest value for both national and international purposes. Nevertheless countries may find that it is not necessary or practicable to include certain of the recommended topics. Their decisions would depend upon their evaluations of how urgently the data were needed, upon resources available, and upon whether information from other sources could be used. . . . The numbers or the order of the topics do not indicate priority or relative importance. . . .

(*a*) *Topics directly based on questionnaire items:*

Geographic items
    (i) Location at time of census and/or place of usual residence

Household or family information
    (ii) Relation to head of household or family

Personal characteristics

(iii) Sex
(iv) Age
(v) Marital status
(vi) Place of birth
(vii) Citizenship

Economic characteristics

(viii) Type of activity
(ix) Occupation
(x) Industry
(xi) Status (as employer, employee, etc.)

Cultural characteristics

(xii) Language
(xiii) Ethnic or nationality characteristics

Education characteristics

(xiv) Literacy
(xv) Level of education
(xvi) School attendance

Fertility data

(xvii) Children—total live-born

(b) *Derived topics*

(xviii) Total population
(xix) Population by size of locality
(xx) Urban-rural classification
(xxi) Household or family composition

'Each country may wish to consider the inclusion of other topics of national value but of lesser universal interest.

'Topics for additional consideration include: prior place of residence, farm or non-farm residence, farm tenure status, number of dependents, type of marriage ceremony, income, secondary occupation, time worked, length of employment or unemployment, household enterprises, professional or vocational education, total number of children born, total number of children living, number of times married, duration of married life, religion and mental and physical disabilities. . . .'

For particular application to Europe these recommendations have been adapted by a Working Party on Population Censuses set up by the Conference of European Statisticians, a representative body of official statisticians which meets under the auspices of the Economic Commission for Europe. Topic (ii) has been replaced by:

> '*Household and family information*
> Relation to main economic supporter (or head) of household.
> Relation to main economic supporter (or head) of family nucleus.'

Topics (xiv) and (xvi) have been omitted from the main list as superfluous (there is little illiteracy in Europe and statistics of school attendance are in many countries derived from the educational system itself), but they have been included in the 'additional topics'. To the group of derived topics the following have been added:

Socio-economic categories.
Dependency relationship.

LESS DEVELOPED COUNTRIES

Historically two conditions have been necessary for the carrying out of a population census:

(a) the economic development of the country has reached a stage at which the degree of urban settlement, literacy and general understanding of central government statistical needs, and communication between localities and the seat of government permit the physical organization of such a relatively sophisticated procedure as the enumeration, even on a minimal scale as a count of heads

(b) the administrative needs of an industrialized society have created such political pressure as to compel the government to seek to impose such a procedure

For the older developed countries this process has taken much longer than for the presently emerging countries which have managed to accelerate their development by learning from, and indeed receiving assistance from, the more advanced countries. For them, condition (b), i.e. the need for demographic information to assist economic planning, has operated before condition (a) has been fully satisfied. In these circumstances the population census has to be carried out in difficult circumstances and must of necessity be more rudimentary than the sophisticated procedure now familiar to Western Society and discussed in this chapter. There is not space in this short manual to deal specifically with the census problems of the less developed countries but we may list them briefly:

(a) Illiteracy or lack of motivation (lack of understanding of the benefit to social administration) may militate against self-enumeration. Skilled interviewers may be required and this will add considerably to the cost of the census

(b) On grounds of cost and/or time it may be necessary to use a sampling method. There will not normally be any ready made person or household sampling frame. It might be necessary to use area sampling. In any case the problems of bias and of grossing-up will be formidable

(c) Concepts such as dwelling, household, marital condition, etc., may be more difficult to define. Much housing will be of a temporary character and rooms as such may not exist. Household or conjugal relationships may be less permanent than in developed countries. Refinement in the description and classification of occupations may be inappropriate; indeed its enforcement could reduce the reliability of the results. Precise ages may not be known and it may be necessary to be content with age-group answers; even these may be approximations or guesses. The term 'level of education' may have no meaning

(d) The distances to be travelled by the census enumerators combined with poor communications may, even where sampling is employed, extend the period of enumeration to the extent that the risk or errors of omission or duplication will be magnified. This is especially likely where the population is nomadic

(e) Lack of advanced data-processing arrangements may limit the scope of the derived tabulations—especially of cross-tabulations. Careful validation of the census returns will be essential before tabulations can commence.

These difficulties are not listed as a deterrent to attempting a census; they provide a caution against over-sophistication. It is clear from the U.N. Demographic Yearbook for 1966 that within these limitations many of the less developed countries co-operated successfully in the World Census Programme 1955–64.

RECENT DEVELOPMENTS IN ANALYSIS OF CENSUS RESULTS

There have been many developments in demographic analyses of census results in recent years and most of them fall within the same broad direction of orientation, namely, the provision of more information about the social and economic characteristics of populations and about the pattern of social and economic organization of communities. The increasing emphasis upon economic aspects of population changes has been an outstanding feature of demography in recent years. In addition there have been new pressures at work. Growing interest in the social stresses of modern industrial development and concomitant urbanization and the relationship between economic and social changes has led to intensified studies into these aspects of sociology, which in turn have brought demands for relevant statistical data.

FERTILITY ANALYSES

Interest in fertility as the most important element in population growth is general. The complexity of the census fertility analyses ranges from the very crude indication given by the ratio of the number of children in the population to the number of women of fertile age, to detailed distributions of family size by marriage age and marriage duration.

In order to assess the pace and direction of changes in family building it is necessary to possess serial sets of fertility rates by age at marriage, calendar year of marriage, and duration of marriage, and, if possible, by birth order. From this information one may see in respect of succeeding marriage cohorts the ultimate size of family likely to be produced and the way in which their fertility is spread over the duration of married life. It is also possible to observe secular changes in the likelihood that a woman who has had, say, two children, will have a third child. Finally, the age-duration fertility rates, if stable or moving in a predictable manner, may be used in connexion with a nuptiality table, to calculate generation replacement rates. The fertility rates are derived from birth registrations and are not themselves census analyses. The role of the census analysis is to provide:

(a) Controls on the intercensal estimation of population at risk
(b) Controls on the year to year estimation of family sizes of which the specific fertility rates form increments

Some rates may be more accurately derived from the census itself. In respect of age, marriage duration, and parity, there is no reason to suppose that at the census the mothers will be differently classified from the way in which, in relation to their offspring, they are classified at birth registration. With regard to socio-economic characteristics (occupations, branch of economic activity, etc.) it is not so; for it is well known that, for example, occupational description may vary significantly not only as between one informant and another but also for the same informant at two different times. This is because a slight change of wording may seriously affect the classification of the occupation.

For this reason an additional question was asked at the 1951 census of England and Wales; married women were asked to indicate whether they had borne a child in the preceding year. In this way fertility rates, specific for occupation, etc., were derived from the census, for which the population at risk (the denominators of the rates) were automatically provided by a single process of classification; the occupation, socio-economic group, etc., *and* the fact of bearing a child within the year of observation (or not doing so) being punched on the same machine card.

HOUSEHOLD AND FAMILY COMPOSITION

The population census is concerned not only with 'counting heads' but with identifying the family and household groupings, i.e. the way in which individual people combine together to satisfy their living needs. This is clearly an essential requirement for understanding the social and economic conditions of the people; it is a part of those conditions, it is a part of the mechanism by which the total national product is created, distributed, and consumed. A knowledge of the life cycle of the growth and disruption of families is necessary for the proper assessment of consumer demand for almost all commodities and especially for estimating housing needs.

The concept of the family is easy to grasp because of its primary biological significance; that of the household, with its economic rather than biological content, is more difficult to define. Because there has been some confusion about both concepts, the Working Group on Censuses of Population and Housing of the E.C.E. Conference of European Statisticians has recommended the following definitions:

A private household[1] may be:

(a) a one-person household, viz. a person who lives alone in a separate housing unit (defined as a structurally separate and independent place of abode) or who occupies, as a lodger, a part or the whole of a separate room or rooms in a part of a housing unit but does not join together with any of the other occupants of the housing unit to form part of a multi-person household as defined below; or

(b) a multi-person household, defined as a group of two or more persons who combine together jointly to occupy the whole or

[1] An institutional household is separately defined as comprising persons 'living in hotels, boarding houses, colleges, schools, hospitals, military installations, penal establishments, who are subject to a common authority or are bound by a common objective and/or personal interests and characteristics.'

part of a housing unit, and to provide themselves with food or other essentials for living. The group may pool their incomes and have a common budget to a greater or lesser extent in different circumstances. The group may be composed of related persons or unrelated persons or a combination of both, including boarders but excluding lodgers.

The basic criteria under this concept of household, which for the sake of convenience may be referred to as the housekeeping unit concept, are that the persons constituting the household jointly occupy a common dwelling space, that they share principal meals (unless prevented for example by working conditions), and that they make a common provision for basic living needs (such as lighting, heating, laundry, etc.). Thus, a multi-person household may be comprised of the members of a family and relatives, resident domestic servants, employees and other persons living with the family as a single house-keeping unit whether or not this group occupies the whole or only a part of a structurally separate dwelling. (It is implicit for this concept that members of the household temporarily absent on census night should be brought within its scope, i.e. we are concerned here with the *de jure* household.)

In the population census it is possible within households to identify families defined as persons who are related by blood, marriage, or adoption. In this definition the marriage relationship includes stable *de facto* unions. The broad concept is of a group or groups of related persons found to be living together within a household. In many cases the family and the household will be identical. There may be different specific concepts according to the object of the statistical analysis. For example, it may be desirable for some purposes to consider:

(a) The family in the narrow sense, limited to a married couple with one or more unmarried children, a married couple without children, or one parent with one or more unmarried children, each of which may be called a 'family nucleus'

(b) The family comprising all the related members of a household

(c) Family relationships extending beyond the household are sometimes considered for sociological or genetic purposes, but this concept of the entire biological family is not suitable for census purposes

For census purposes the primary unit is the family nucleus because it is the unit which most facilitates analysis of family and household structure.

It is important to bear in mind that there is a clear methodological distinction between the household and the family (as defined above). The household is identified by the census enumerator; the family, as such, is not identified by the enumerator but is fixed mechanically during the data processing on the basis of information written into the census schedule in respect of all members of the household. It is therefore more natural to proceed from households to families. It will also be important to bear in mind that a classification of households will to some extent involve a classification of family components of households.

The head of the household is usually considered in the conduct of the census to be that person who is acknowledged as such by the other household members. It is more important for purposes of household composition and dependency statistics, however, to identify the person on whom falls the chief responsibility for the economic maintenance of the household, i.e. the main breadwinner or the principal contributor to the household budget, who may be called the 'main economic supporter'. The identification requires either a direct question in the census schedule or the establishment of criteria, e.g. economic activity, socio-economic category, sex, seniority of age, etc., by means of which a choice is made during the data-processing.

The same approach can also be made in relation to the family nucleus. This gives rise to the concepts of the head of the family nucleus and the supporter of such a family. Often these persons are identical; and when the household comprises only one family nucleus, the analysis of the household coincides with that of the family.

Households may be classified first according to whether they constitute private or institutional households. Private households can then be classified into non-family, one-family, and multi-family households (the latter may be further subdivided according to the number of family nuclei they contain). *Non-family households* may be classified into one-person and multi-person households; the multi-person households may be further subdivided into those consisting of related persons only, of related and unrelated persons, and of unrelated persons only. Distinction could also be made between direct descent and other relationship (for example between a grandfather and a grandchild on the one hand and two sisters on the other). *One-family* households may be classified into the following types:

(a) A married couple with one or more unmarried children
(b) A married couple without children
(c) One parent with one or more unmarried children

Each of these types of family nucleus may be combined with other persons either related, unrelated, or both within the household. *Multi-family households* are classified according to whether or not any of the family nuclei are related and whether or not this relationship is in direct descent; in addition, the family nuclei themselves may be classified by type as already indicated for those in one-family households. The number of possible combinations of axes of classification is therefore large, and it has been suggested that, though full analysis may have to be undertaken on occasions, for most practical purposes the analysis of households (as distinct from families) would be facilitated if each multi-family household could be typified by a *primary family* within it. This primary family could be selected on the basis of criteria related to the object of the analysis. For example, it could be the family nucleus with the oldest head, or the family nucleus containing the main economic supporter of the household, etc. The breakdown of a large household in accordance with the principles outlined above is shown in Table Four.

TABLE FOUR

A three-family household

No.	Name	Relationship to head	Sex Age	Marital condition	Occupation	Chief economic supporter	
						House-hold	Family
1.	Henry Brown	Head[1]	M. 65	Married	Retired farmer		
2.	Emily Brown	Spouse	F. 60	Married	Housewife		
3.	George Brown	Son	M. 42	Single	Farm Mgr.	X	X
4.	Helen Brown	Daughter	F. 39	Single	House duties		
5.	John Smith	Brother-in-law	M. 62	Single	Carpenter (non-agric.)		
6.	James Robinson	Employee	M. 60	Single	Farm worker	———	
7.	Eric Brown	Son	M. 40	Married	Welder (non-agric.)		X
8.	Joan Brown	Daughter-in-law	F. 38	Married	Housewife		
9.	David Brown	Grandson	M. 10	—	—		
10.	Jane Jones	Sister-in-law	F. 50	Widow	Family worker (farm)	———	X
11.	Mary Jones	Niece-in-law	F. 30	Single	Teacher		

Primary family nucleus: [1 + 2 + 3 + 4]
(Note that 5 and 6 though related and unrelated respectively are *not* part of the family)
Secondary family nuclei: [7 + 8 + 9] in direct descent and [10 + 11] not in direct descent
Dependent on agriculture: economically inactive [1 + 2 + 4]; economically active [3 + 6 + 10]
Dependent on other industry: economically inactive [8 + 9 + 11]; economically active [5 + 7]

[1] Head in the conventional sense of accepting responsibility for the census schedule.

The analysis of families is best undertaken in terms of family nuclei. Just as in household analysis the development is from households to the family nuclei of which they are composed and which serve to differentiate the households, so it is necessary in family analysis to proceed from different types of family nuclei to their disposition within the households into which they are integrated. For completeness, it should be borne in mind that family nuclei living as members of institutional households have to be included. Thus, in the first place, it is necessary to identify the three types of family nuclei, living in both private and institutional households. Secondly, the family nuclei living in private households are classified according to whether they are in one-family, two-family, three-family, etc., households. Where for the purpose of household analysis certain family nuclei have been designated as primary families and the others as secondary families, this designation provides a further axis of classification.

These household classifications are relatively simple and capable of further development, as indeed has been the case in some countries, notably in the Federal Republic of Germany, where they have introduced the interesting concept of the 'functional scope of households', i.e. for each individual the extent to which he participates in the basic functions of the household, for example, by:

(a) Sharing meals which are prepared for the household in common

(b) Having laundry washed together with that of the total household

(c) Contributing to a common budget from which the requirements of daily life are financed

This clearly provides a further measure of the cohesion of households and an additional axis of classification.

Cross-tabulations from the basic bution distriof household or family types would show for each type the number of persons in the household, the number and ages of children, and the number of earners and income recipients.

Another type of analysis that has been developed involves classifying households by the social and economic characteristics of a principal member, e.g. the chief economic supporter of the household. The characteristics cover a wide range and include occupancy of dwelling (as owner or tenants), level of education, type of activity, occupation, branch of economic activity, employment status, socioeconomic group, as well as sex, age, and marital status.

HOUSING

To the census authority, dwellings and people are inseparable in the sense that it is difficult and very largely meaningless to measure housing resources without relating those resources to their present as well as their potential use. It is therefore customary in most countries to conduct the housing census simultaneously with, and as an integral part of, the population census. On the one hand, this enables housing data to be classified in relation to the characteristics of the population accommodated in the dwelling units (as a means of assessing the adequacy of housing), and on the other hand, it makes it possible to classify the population in relation to their housing (as a means of measuring both current levels of living and potential housing demand).

Analytical developments have taken the form of more detailed cross-tabulations between household structural groups and classifications of types of housing accommodation. It is now regarded as inadequate to classify housing units merely according to the number of rooms they contain. A number of new axes of classification have been introduced.

In the first place there has been some standardization, as a result of United Nations guidance, in the classification of housing units,[1] viz.:

(a) Private housing units:

    (i) Conventional (permanent) dwellings (house, apartment, flat, etc.)

    (ii) Rustic (semi-permanent) units, e.g. huts, cabins, etc., and improved units, e.g. shacks

    (iii) Mobile housing units, e.g. trailers, caravans, boats, etc.

(b) Collective housing units (designed for occupancy by two or more households or by an institutional household):

    (i) Hotels and boarding houses

    (ii) Institutions, e.g. hospitals, boarding schools, barracks

    (iii) Camps, e.g. lumber camps or military camps without fixed location

There is also a need to classify the type of building structure in which the housing units are situated. There is the question whether it is a residential building or a non-residential building (commercial, industrial, etc.). In many countries owing to a general shortage of housing there has been a rapid increase in the provision of flats, both by new building and by the conversion of existing large houses.

---

[1] 'An independent room, group of rooms, apartment, flat or house *designed* for habitation by a private or institutional household *or* a boat, wagon, hut, cave or any other structure *occupied* as living quarters.'

The period of construction may also be recorded as an indicator of obsolescence.

A further axis for cross-tabulation is the tenure as owner-occupier, tenant, or sub-tenant. (This may also be regarded as an economic characteristic of the household.)

The main characteristics of the housing unit to be tabulated within the type-groups discussed above are:

(a) Size, i.e. number of rooms
(b) Number of occupying households, and persons
(c) Facilities (water supply, toilet, bath, ventilation, etc.)
(d) Social and economic characteristics of head of household

Commonly (a) and (b) are crossed (to give density of housing for each household size) within each housing unit type.

Recent developments in housing analyses have been attempts to examine the housing of special sections of the population (for example, old people living alone or certain specified household structures); estimates of the adequacy or inadequacy of the existing stock of housing on various hypotheses as to the space needs of different household (and family) structures; studies of the sharing of dwellings in terms of the structural types of household which combine to share: studies of obsolescence (as indicated by lack of facilities or evidence of conversion from original design).

DEPENDENCY

In keeping with the new economic emphasis in demography much attention has been given to the classification of the population according to their mode of participation in the economy. A simple classification by type of economic activity has been drawn up as follows:

(a) *Economically active population*
   (i) Employed
   (ii) Unemployed

(b) *Inactive population*
   (i) With income

      (A) Former members of active population (i.e. pensioners deriving their subsistence from former activity)
      (B) Living on income from capital, State aid, etc.

   (ii) Without income, i.e. dependents

      (A) Students
      (B) Home houseworkers

(c) Persons in institutions

(d) Other adults in the home

Since it is the active population who provide the goods and services which are consumed by all, it is an important part of long-term economic planning to assess, from a total population point of view, the likely trend in the numerical relationship between the inactive and active populations.

The same kind of study is of importance at the household and more particularly at the family level for the purpose of measuring the economic strength of different structures. The problem is to attach the dependent members of the family to the member or members upon whom they are dependent. The supporters may be further classified to show not only the numbers of their dependents but also the sector of economy or branch of economic activity on which they, the supporters, are in turn dependent.

It is important to note that the analyses of household and family structure, and of dependency, are problems of arrangement of data already on the census schedule; they do not involve specific questions except that, in the case of dependency, a question is needed to identify income recipients.

INCOME

As distinct from analyses of dependency which are concerned with the presence or absence of incomes, there has been little development in the direction of analysing incomes by size. As a result it has been necessary in the study of levels of living to turn to a battery of indicators such as food consumption, infant mortality, education facilities. Some countries have carried out household income and expenditure surveys on an hoc basis but not as part of the population census, so that it is only possible to cross-tabulate with a limited number of other social and economic characteristics.

It has to be borne in mind that household budget inquiries of the *continuous* sample survey type provide constantly up-to-date information in circumstances of prices and wages which are always changing, and this is a strong balance of advantage in favour of the survey method.

OCCUPATION AND BRANCH OF ECONOMIC ACTIVITY

Tabulations indicating the distribution of skills in the labour force and the apportionment of the labour force among the different branches of economic activity are of fundamental importance to labour recruitment and mobility, to measurement of the development of branches of economic activity, and to an appreciation of the economic characteristics of population groups. The general interest in the provision of comparable statistics for international comparative studies of economic development is evident from the establishment of international standard classifications of other occupation (I.S.C.O.) and branch of economic activity (I.S.I.C.) There are also international recommendations on the subsidiary classification of the active population by employment status, viz.:

     Employers
     Workers on own account
     Employees
     Family workers
     Members of producer's co-operatives

New developments in analyses have been less in the direction of elaborating the basic distributions of occupation and industrial groups by sex, age, and employment status, than in cross-tabulation with other characteristics such as housing, education, or fertility, or household structure. There is nevertheless a growing recognition of the scope for meaningful subdivision of skill and function within the framework of minimal standard classifications. Most broad occupational groupings are concerned with separating managers, non-manual workers, skilled, semi-skilled, and unskilled workmen. Not only are the assignments to these groups somewhat arbitrary but the groups themselves are large, unwieldy, and heterogeneous. It seems likely that either by utilizing non-census data on types of training required (especially distinguishing re-employment from in-service training) or by cross-tabulation with census data on education, duration of employment, and employment status, it might be possible to break up these groups into an approximation to levels of skill, or responsibility.

There is considerable interest in the separation of the managerial element in industry; in the distinction between the makers of policy and those who, albeit with some elbow-room of discretion, merely carry out a prescribed policy. The relationship of the managerial to the non-managerial labour force in different industries throws light upon the development of the organizational structure. Here again a single group of managers is too large and heterogeneous, and splits are made according to branch of economic activity (agriculture, extractive industry, productive industry, distribution, government, etc.) and also by size of establishment (total number of workers). With regard to this latter factor of size it would, of course, be more meaningful to classify managers by the number of workers they manage, but this would require a specific question, and it would be naïve to expect reliable answers. If 'manager' is incorporated into the employment status classification as well as in the classification of occupations, then a single tabulation of the economically active by branch of economic activity and status is sufficient for all these purposes. Such a tabulation shows, for example, from one census to another, the trend in the proportion of 'own account' workers (a downward trend indicating the organization of industry in larger units) and in the incidence of the 'family worker' status as a general indicator of economic development.

In order to provide information relating to the inter-industry or inter-occupation (as distinct from geographical) mobility of labour, as a background to the assessment of economic stability or flexibility, tabulations may usefully be made of 'duration of present employment' (in relation to age). Such a distribution shows to what extent labour is mobile and to what extent the occupation and industries recorded may be regarded as 'usual'. Another kind of tabulation which is partly related to labour mobility is that of secondary occupations. This is only relevant to countries where there are significant numbers of workers with more than one occupation, either simultaneously, or consecutively within a short time interval; to every secondary occupation there would also be a secondary industry and a secondary employment status. To be useful the tabulation must be presented as a cross-tabulation of primary and secondary occupations (and industries), and this is a formidable undertaking.

Another aspect of labour statistics, in respect of which in some countries there is a tendency to regard the population census as the source, is that of hours of employment per week. A tabulation showing a distribution of hours of work for each occupation and industry provides an indication of relative working conditions in different avenues of employment; furnishes information on under-employment where it exists; and serves to provide standards for regulating social security schemes. For this latter purpose it is useful also to have tabulations of frequency and method of payment.

Socio-economic Grouping

One of the most interesting of modern developments in demographic analyses, and one which illustrates forcefully the increased emphasis upon economic aspects of population statistics, has been the production of socio-economic groupings. In order to observe the inter-relationship of population trends (in the wider sense which embraces cultural and behavioural changes) and economic factors, it is necessary to divide the population into groups which are homogeneous in respect of the level of living (in material terms), educational background, and social attitude.

Two alternative approaches have been made. The first method is to attribute to each of the occupations distinguished in the classification a ranking based either on social values, for example that of standing within the community (such as in the United Kingdom from the 1911 census onward[1]), or a score derived from a battery of such values. This has two disadvantages:

(a) There is a likelihood that the ranking will be influenced by preconceived notions of just those differentials of health or behaviour which the groupings are to be used to discover

(b) It is difficult to provide an economic interpretation of the ultimate inter-relationships of the groups and other social characteristics because of the abstract and subjective character of the ranking

A second method has therefore been developed which is of a much more objective character in that it is derived automatically from a cross-tabulation of the four economic classifications already referred to, viz:

(a) Type of activity in the economy
(b) Occupation
(c) Employment status
(d) Branch of economic activity (industry)

The individual cells of such a cross-tabulation represent groups with substantial homogeneity of social and economic characteristics, and these can be gathered into broader groups to the extent of contraction in numbers of groups that may be desired. An important feature of these groups is the fact that they are not necessarily ranked in any preconceived order; it is claimed only that they are economically *different*, not that one group has higher social standing than another. Clearly in material terms the level of living is higher for one group than another, so that some degree of economic ordering is inevitable.

The European Working Group on Population Census of E.C.E. has subjected this system to close study and has recommended the following combinations:

[1] Under this system which is still in use, especially for occupational mortality purposes, every occupation (and therefore every person who follows it) is assigned to one of five social classes (really occupational classes), viz., (i) Professional, etc., (ii) Intermediate, (iii) Skilled workers, (iv) Partly skilled workers, (v) Unskilled workers.

Socio-economic Classification

(a) *Economically active population*

    (i) Farm-employers
    (ii) Farmers on own account without employees
    (iii) Members of agricultural producers' co-operatives
    (iv) Agricultural workers
    (v) Employers in industry and commerce; large enterprises
    (vi) Employers in industry and commerce; small enterprises
    (vii) Employers in industry and commerce; own account workers without employees
    (viii) Liberal and related professions
    (ix) Members of non-agricultural producers' co-operatives
    (x) Directors (managers) of enterprises and companies
    (xi) Senior non-manual workers
    (xii) Intermediate and junior non-manual workers and sales workers
    (xiii) Supervisors and skilled, semi-skilled and specialized manual workers
    (xiv) Labourers
    (xv) Service staff (domestic servants, cleaners, caretakers) and related workers
    (xvi) Members of armed forces on compulsory military service
    (xvii) Economically active persons not classifiable in the above groups

(b) *Economically inactive population*

    (xviii) Former farm-employers
    (xix) Former non-agricultural employers
    (xx) Former employees
    (xxi) Other independent inactive persons
    (xxii) Children below minimum school-leaving age
    (xxiii) Students and school-children above minimum school-leaving age
    (xxiv) Housewives
    (xxv) Other adults in the home
    (xxvi) Inmates of institutions

(Further subdivisions were suggested, and also summary groups, but these have been omitted in the interests of brevity.)

These socio-economic groups may then be used to classify the whole population (attributing to dependents the groups of those on whom they are dependent) or the active population only, or whole households (by the group of the chief economic supporter).

As in the case of the analysis of household structure, this socio-economic grouping is essentially a matter of exploiting information already provided on the census schedule; it does not involve additional specific questions. In the 1961 census and subsequently in Great Britain a broad classification in seventeen socio-economic groups based on these principles has been adopted. They are defined in the introduction to the published occupation classification 1960.

Sector of the Economy

As has already been demonstrated, the economic information provided on the census schedule may be organized in a number of different ways. One additional way is to divide the active population between the public and private sectors of the economy by reference to branch of economic activity, occupation, and employment status. This is particularly of interest in countries where it is desired to observe the extent and pace of socialization of industry. Such an analysis is also of importance in any planned economy where it is desired, for example, to maintain a balanced programme of expansion as between the different sectors and it is necessary to observe the related man-power problems.

Workplace

Where many people live in one locality and work in another, as in the United Kingdom, the geographical distribution of numbers of workers in different branches of economic activity has to be carried out on the basis of the area in which the workplace is situated as distinct from the area of residence of the worker. Since, in these circumstances, the address of residence and the address of the workplace are both recorded on the one schedule it is possible to attach area codes to these addresses and to carry out two types of analysis:

(a) Measurement of the difference between the day and night populations of urban localities and an examination of the character of the net inward movement each day and its distribution by sex, age, occupation, etc.

(b) A cross-tabulation of area of residence and area of workplace to indicate the broad lines of journey (since the tabulation has to be in terms of persons crossing administrative area boundaries, movements *within* an administrative area are excluded and long and short movements across the boundary are given equal weight)[1]

[1] More recently the General Register Office has made tabulations in more detail using smaller areal units than local authority areas.

These analyses are of value to transport authorities who want to know the number of people to be moved and the social and economic characteristics of those who journey to work; and to town planning authorities who have to consider whether such movement is tolerable or could be avoided by re-siting industry or residential centres, or both. An increasing volume of movement to work is also of interest as indicating the later stage of town development in which the mixed market, residential, and cultural core is displaced by the growing commercial centre; and when both the diminishing residential accommodation and the noise and atmospheric pollution of expanding factory and office areas compel workers to seek dwellings in more open spaces on the periphery of the town.

Internal Migration

Of more general importance is the urbanization which accompanies industrialization in all countries and which, in many, results in large internal migratory movements of population. In turn this migration may have extensive demographic effects in changing population structure in different parts of the country and in producing mortality and fertility differentials. Even where economic development is already advanced, there are streams of movement the direction and pace of which are of interest to administrative bodies. Internal migration has become, again as part of the economic orientation in population studies, an important topic of demographic analysis. In many countries questions of the type 'Were you living at this address a year ago? If so, how long have you lived here? If not, what was the address of your usual residence a year ago?' have been introduced into the population census.

Movements may be classified by the type—for example, rural to rural, rural to urban, urban to rural; within the same region and outside the region of former residence. These movement types may then be cross-tabulated with sex, age, occupation, branch of economic activity, socio-economic group, and household and family structure. There can also be a cross-tabulation of area of present residence and area of former residence, so as to show up the main streams of movement taking place within the country. Further, the movers themselves may be treated as a selected population and a special study can be made of their social and economic characteristics.

Urban and Rural Population

The present stage of development of the continual urbanization which has been taking place may be gauged by separating the population into urban and rural elements and examining the size and disposition of the clusters of population.

This involves establishing conventions for the identification of population clusters. The most practical method is to work with large-scale maps which reveal street formation and the disposition of scattered buildings. The population of such street formations or scattered buildings which are not separated by more than a specified distance may be regarded as comprising one cluster. For this purpose administrative boundaries are ignored,[1] as the concept of the cluster is quite distinct from that of the local authority area. The clusters and any residual scattered buildings are then grouped into *localities*, i.e. population groups forming a unity indicated by social and economic interdependence in their daily lives. Localities may then be classified as urban or rural on the basis of population size and the distribution of the active population by industry. The criterion of size of population can be used to distinguish three categories consisting of small, medium-sized, and large localities. Some countries use 2000 as the dividing line between the first two categories and 10,000 as the dividing line between the second and third.

A second criterion of industrial activity can be used to distinguish within the smallest size-group between agricultural and non-agricultural localities. These localities in which the proportion of the active population engaged in agriculture exceeds say twenty per cent would be classed as rural agricultural localities and the others as rural non-agricultural localities.

This would mean that four basic categories would be distinguished, namely, rural agricultural, rural non-agricultural, intermediate, and urban localities.

The next stage in classification would be to break down the heterogeneous intermediate category, either by the application of the simple criterion of the proportion of the active population engaged in agriculture, or by the separation of the proportions engaged in agriculture, industry, and service activities or, if the necessary data be available, by reference to such criteria as the presence of an administration centre, the type of building (one-storey or multi-storey), availability of hospitals, etc. Localities can also be classified according to their functional type (industrial centre, university centre, holiday resort, etc.).

---

[1] It should be borne in mind that we are dealing here with a special purpose, and not a complete alternative to administrative areas which must still form the basis of the main census tabulations.

Education

The extent to which education and employment are correctly matched is of immense importance to the attainment of high levels of productivity. Definition of standards of instruction must inevitably be in terms of the administration of the educational system of the country concerned, and they will probably only have meaning within the context of that system. The analyses then take the form of cross-tabulations of standards of instruction with occupation, branch of economic activity, status, socio-economic group, and with other characteristics such as housing, family structure, and fertility.

Structure of Census Analyses

The main structure of census analyses can be set out systematically as follows:

Units	Axes
Person	Sex, age, marital condition, fertility, birthplace, nationality, education, economic activity, occupation, industry, workplace, migration
Family	Structural type, situation in household, economic strength (ratio of economically active to dependent members)
Household	Structural type, family content, economic strength characteristics of chief economic supporter, housing
Locality (cluster)	Size, industrial character, urban/rural division, function
Administrative area	Principal aggregate of tabulation

Organization of the Census

The census is taken on a particular day, at intervals of several years, of a population which is not only continually changing in total size, but is also changing in constitution (age, sex, occupation, etc.) and in its geographical disposition within the national boundary. In times of industrial crisis or of mobilization of military forces, violent changes may be taking place; on a minor level, sharp changes in regional distribution occur in the usual holiday seasons. It would be ideal therefore to fix a time at which such changes are minimal, so that on the one hand the actual enumeration may be facilitated by stable conditions, and on the other the results may be more likely to reflect the average condition of the population about the time of the census, i.e. the census will be representative of that era and intercensal changes will typify broad trends rather than sharp and often transient fluctuations. Choice of census year is largely determined, however, by considerations of continuity and regularity, such as the desirability of maintaining equal decennial intervals from the first census in Britain in 1801 and in America from 1790.

In any particular year the day chosen should be such as to find most people at their usual occupation and in their usual residence, so as to narrow the gap between *de facto* and *de jure* enumerations. While it is desirable to choose a week-end out of the holiday season so as to minimize absences from home for holiday, social, or business reasons, it is also desirable to carry out the enumeration at a time of the year when the weather is not inclement and the evenings are light so as to facilitate the task of the enumerators. There are statistical advantages in choosing a date near the middle of the year so that little adjustment is needed to produce a mid-year estimate. In Britain the choice of a Sunday in April is a compromise which attempts to take account of all these considerations.

If as in some countries the enumeration is spread over a period of weeks rather than made on a single day, certain problems are created. Some persons who move during the enumeration period may be missed altogether, since the area in which they originally lived may not be canvassed before they move and enumeration may be completed in the area of their new home by the time they arrive; there is equally the possibility of double enumeration. Furthermore, enumerators tend to ignore the nominal date of enumeration and to record information as at the date of the visit; in spite of instructions it is found that some infants are included in the census though born after the census date, and some persons who died after the census date are excluded. The fact that in Britain a householder completes the schedule, instead of giving answers to an interviewer, enables a simultaneous count to be taken in all parts of the country on a single day and thus avoids these difficulties.

Enumeration Districts

The method of enumeration in Great Britain is basically simple though the administrative task is monumental. The country is split up into districts the boundaries of which are carefully defined and the area of which can be covered from dwelling to dwelling by the enumerator (recruited part-time for the task) within two days at most. These districts are sub-divisions of registration districts and local registration staff traditionally become supervising census officers for the duration of the enumeration; by the same token the enumeration districts add up to local authority areas. Questionnaires (schedules) to be completed by the householder are distributed a few days before census day and are collected as quickly as possible after that date, a large proportion on the day following. Enumerators are briefed and are equipped with instruction manuals to enable them to identify separate dwellings and households and to deal with difficulties of interpretation of the schedule. Enumerators check that the schedules are complete and pass them on to the local census officers who inspect them again before transmitting them to census headquarters for data processing.

De facto *and* de jure *populations*

A person may for purposes of local enumeration be recorded according to usual residence (*de jure*) as in America, or according to where he is at the time of the census (*de facto*) as in Great Britain. For many purposes it is desirable to have *de jure* tabulations; for example, if the local populations are to be used for the calculation of birth and death rates and birth and death registration is on a *de jure* basis as in Great Britain. On the other hand, where the schedule is to be completed by the head of the household, it is clearly simpler to request the enumeration of all persons in the household at the time of the census; it avoids awkward distinctions between permanent and temporary residence, and the special treatment of instances where, for example, a family live in one house in the summer and another in the winter. The *de facto* enumeration is least satisfactory in health resorts and other districts where transient waves of migration periodically occur. In most areas of Britain, since the census takes place everywhere in a single night (so that no person can be enumerated in two places) and at a time of year when holiday movement is minimal, the two populations do not differ greatly.

In recent censuses in Great Britain though the enumeration has been conducted on a *de facto* basis (the persons actually in the dwelling) questions have also been asked about the *de jure* (normal) constitution of the household so that at least tabulation of *de jure* size distributions could be produced.

Errors in Census Data

In spite of publicity about the nature of the questions to be answered on the schedule, and of care taken in the framing of the questions, there may be persons who do not understand the questions, who do not trouble to ascertain the precise answer, or find the official concepts unacceptable. Inaccuracy in a population census cannot be entirely eliminated.

Error in the total number of persons enumerated is probably small. After the 1921 census it was stated (in the Preliminary Report) that a population estimate at census date, built up from the 1911 census population but based only on provisional migration statistics, exceeded the provisional 1921 count, of nearly 38 million, by 33,000, or less than 1 per 1000, though later examination suggested that the difference was a little greater. At the 1931 census the estimate carried through the intercensal period to 1931 was less than the enumerated population by barely $\frac{1}{2}$ per 1000, though this agreement was admitted to be fortuitously close. After the 1951 census it was stated that an estimate at census date exceeded the final count of nearly 44 million by 134,000, a difference of less than 3 per 1000. These comparisons are not a true test of census coverage. The estimates involved are built up from the base population with recorded births and deaths and estimated migrants, the latter being much less accurately assessed than the other elements. The comparisons are thus primarily a test of migration estimates, but, since errors in the latter could account for the whole of the differences revealed, they do at least suggest that any error in census coverage is quite trivial, and certainly too slight to be measured by the available standards.

In fact in 1961 the census total was greater by some 40,000 than the projected estimate; this illustrates the weakness of the test.

A particular feature of any short fall, and one which commonly occurs and is easy to recognize, is a deficiency of very young infants as compared with those expected from recent birth registrations after allowing for mortality. In 1921, 795,000 infants aged nought and 826,000 infants aged one were enumerated, compared with 819,000 and 848,000 expected from registration records, a total error for the two ages of 46,000. It was thought that the error arose from difficulty in entering on the census schedule newly born children who were unchristened or unnamed. In 1931 therefore a note was inserted to the effect that such infants should be described as 'baby'. As a result the error was reduced to 13,000–11,000 at age nought and 2000 at age one. In 1951 the corresponding deficiencies were 14,000 and 12,000, and in 1961, 11,000 and 12,000.

When the age distribution of an enumerated population is examined a distinctive type of irregularity often becomes obvious; there are inordinately large numbers returned at ages with certain digital endings, especially nought and eight, but sometimes at five. It may be that where there is uncertainty as to age there is a tendency to approximate to the nearest ten or to an even number close to a multiple of ten. In addition there is an error arising from the fact that those within a short period of a birthday tend to return the higher age instead of the attained age. These errors have decreased at successive censuses. At earlier censuses there was some evidence (based on a comparison of the enumerated population with that derived from past births, allowing for mortality and migration) that females tended to understate their ages when approaching middle age. There has been much less evidence of this in recent censuses.

The recording of occupations is subject to errors or defects of three kinds: (i) there is a tendency to elevate the status, e.g. an unskilled labourer may describe himself in terms suggesting special skill, and some persons describe themselves as working in a supervisory capacity when they have no such responsibility; (ii) a man who has been out of work for some time or who has been forced to change his occupation temporarily may quote his former occupation if he is likely to return to it, or his temporary occupation if he thinks it is likely to become his permanent means of livelihood; at a time of widespread unemployment this could seriously misrepresent the true industrial pattern; (iii) some of the older unoccupied or retired persons, especially those who have preferred, and still hope, to continue work, return themselves as engaged in their old occupations.

The incidence of these various errors is not precisely known, and in past censuses could only be surmised from anomalies in the tabulations and from various consistency tests. The general impression is that self-enumeration can be combined with a high standard of accuracy. In general it is considered prudent to carry out, in advance of the full enumeration, a small-scale sample test census combined with interviewer call-back to establish not only the nature and incidence of errors but also the reasons for their occurrence. From information thus gathered it is possible, by improvements in schedule design or variations in the form of the questions, to minimize the incidence of errors in the full enumeration. Further, the residual incidence of errors is measured by a sample post-enumeration survey, again conducted by call-back interview. In this way a 'quality label' can be attached to the census tabulations. From 1966 this has become standard practice in Great Britain. For a full account of the various types of inaccuracy to which the census may be subject reference should be made to the general reports on the successive censuses published by the Registrar General of England and Wales.

Editing

It is not proposed to go into detail of data processing except to stress that the use of electronic computers makes it possible to 'clean' the records before tabulations commence. The computer is programmed to inspect each record for specified internal inconsistencies or impossible characteristics (age 150, male 'mothers', ordained priest age twelve, etc.) and on finding such an 'error' to both mark the tape record as suspect and print out the nature of the query. Reference can then be made to the original record. Fresh

records are then written in to the original data tapes either confirming or correcting the earlier record. In some cases the computer can be programmed to follow specified rules for automatic correction. For example in the event of age being unrecorded an age could be selected (having regard to marital status and whether employed or at school, etc.) from a possible range. For further details reference should be made to the General Reports on the census of 1961 and to computer literature.

REFERENCES

The published reports of national censuses contain much of methodological interest as well as providing source material on a wide range of demographic topics.

Guides to Official Sources No. 2, Census Reports of Great Britain 1801–1931. Interdepartmental Committee on Social and Economic Research. (1951).

Handbook on Population Census Methods: Volume I, General Aspects of a Population Census; Volume II, Economic Characteristics of the Population; and Volume III, Demographic and Social Characteristics of the Population. United Nations Statistical Office (1965).

5

Fertility measurement

FERTILITY measures the rate at which a population adds to itself by births and is normally assessed by relating the number of births to the size of some section of the population, such as the number of married couples or the numbers of women of child-bearing age, i.e. an appropriate yardstick of potential fertility. The number of births, though determined by attitudes toward family size, is limited by the number of women exposed to the risk of pregnancy and, in the consideration of fertility measures, the choice of the population at risk is important.

FERTILITY VARIATION

Since some ninety-three per cent of all births in England and Wales are legitimate, the extent to which people marry at any time exercises a powerful influence on the subsequent flow of births. The number of couples who marry will depend upon the available numbers and the relative age distributions of men and women within the marriageable age period and these will depend upon antecedent births (and the marriage experience producing them); thus future fertility depends upon past fertility. Though there are thus these quantitative restraints on the variation of fertility, there is also an important element of unpredictable fluctuation due to changes in attitude. More widespread knowledge of contraceptive methods and the introduction of more efficient methods have, in this country as in many other developed countries, resulted in an approach to a state of fertility control, i.e. a state of close approximation of achievement to intention. The gap between attained family size and desired family size is very small. Fertility is now therefore much more sensitive to social and economic changes affecting attitudes to family size. Stable trends of fertility over long periods are not to be expected and long term forecasts of fertility are subject to wide margins of error.

Factors Affecting Fertility Variation

The number of children produced by a group of women in a given year will depend upon their ages, whether they are married, how long they have been married and how many children they have already borne. It will depend also upon the economic resources, housing conditions and the educational facilities available. It may also depend upon where they live, e.g. whether in an urban or a rural environment.

Birth Rate

The crude birth rate is usually calculated by relating total live births in a year to the total population of all ages and expressing it as a rate per 1000. The total population is not the proper population at risk so far as births are concerned since it contains males, and also females outside the child-bearing ages. The crude birth rate is satisfactory only when the true number exposed to risk is a fixed proportion of the total population, i.e. when it is used for the same community in a short series of years, or in comparing the birth rates of communities whose populations are known to be nearly, if not quite, equal in their age and sex composition and in marital condition. If, however, the number of women, especially of married women, of child-bearing age changes in the one community studied or differs in two populations compared, the crude birth rate will vary from this cause apart from true fertility variations. However misleading as a measure of fertility, the crude birth rate does measure the gross rate of increase of the population by births.

Fertility Rate

The *general fertility rate* is obtained by expressing the live births as a rate per 1000 of women of child-bearing age, taken as either 15–49 or 15–44. The difficulty is that, although this rate is properly related to the population at risk, it requires estimates of the female population by age and marital status in inter-censal years and for small local areas this may involve more error than would be entailed in using crude birth rates for comparison. It is possible to introduce some correction to birth rates for differences in population age structure. An area comparability factor may be calculated which represents the ratio of an 'expected' birth rate—obtained by applying standard (usually national) fertility rates by age to the local population structure—to the actual rate recorded in the standard population. If this factor is above/below unity it indicates that the local rate must be correspondingly reduced/increased to allow for departure from standard population structure. If local birth rates in inter-censal years are multiplied by the appropriate census-based factors the rates thus adjusted are comparable. This is the method used by the Registrar General for England and Wales.

Area Comparability Factors

Area comparability factors for use with birth rates were introduced in 1949. The present series of A.C.F.s used by the Registrar General are effectively indirect standardizing factors and are based on the sex and age composition of the population as determined by the most recent population census.

Effectively if P_x is the number of women in the population aged x to $x + 4$; and P is the total population of all ages and both sexes; f_x is the group fertility rate for women aged x to $x + 4$; and accents indicate local area figures, national figures being unaccented, we require, as an indirect standardizing factor to adjust the crude local birth rate,

$$\frac{\Sigma f_x . P_x/P}{\Sigma f_x . P_x'/P'}$$

This is, as it should be, greater than unity if the local age structure is such that P_x'/P_x is relatively lower at the younger ages where fertility rates are higher, i.e. if the local population is relatively deficient of women at child bearing ages. But since $\Sigma f_x . P_x/P$ is the persons all ages rate R for England and Wales, then the expression may be written $\Sigma \dfrac{P'}{(f_x/R) . P_x'}$, a form which facilitates computation.

Thus in accordance with this expression the procedure is as follows:

The child-bearing component of the population of England and Wales, taken for this purpose as women aged 15–44, is separated into six five-year age groups (viz., 15–19, 20–24, etc.). Group birth rates are then obtained by dividing the number of live births occurring to mothers in each age group during the triennium surrounding the census by three times the corresponding census population. The group rates are then each divided by a rate for persons of all ages, calculated on a similar basis to the group rates but using total live births and total population, to give a series of group weighting factors. To obtain the A.C.F. for any given area the Census female population in each of the six age groups is multiplied by the appropriate weighting factor and the products accumulated. The total population of the area divided by the result gives the area comparability factor.

It should be kept in mind that the A.C.F. for any given area relates to the population of the area as defined by the boundaries existing at the time of the most recent census. Provided that in the meantime there are no changes in boundary or other population movement (e.g. special housing or New Town development) important enough to disturb appreciably the relative sex and age distribution of the

3

population included, the A.C.F. will remain applicable until a new series of factors can be calculated on the basis of the next census. Where an area is affected by the special changes referred to, the A.C.F. is recalculated on the basis of the most up-to-date knowledge of the movements involved.

Legitimacy

Where possible it is appropriate to sub-divide the general fertility rate into two components, (1) the ratio of legitimate births to married women 15–49 and (2) the ratio of illegitimate births to unmarried women 15–49. This secures a better relationship between births and exposed to risk but even so it is not a precise method. If a marriage takes place during pregnancy, the birth is registered as legitimate and this tends to reduce the true illegitimate fertility and to increase the legitimate component. If a married man dies before his child is born the birth is legitimate and appears in the numerator of (1) while the mother as a widow appears in the denominator of (2). Broadly, however, an accurate picture is obtained.

Illegitimacy is commonly expressed by calculating illegitimate births as a *percentage of total live births*. Though satisfactory when applied to short term comparisons this method may be misleading over a long term for if the legitimate birth rate were declining and the illegitimate birth rate were constant, the percentage illegitimacy would show an increase. The percentage illegitimacy may fluctuate considerably when war conditions disturb normal relationships.

MULTIPLE BIRTHS

Owing to the occurrence of twins, triplets and higher orders of multiple deliveries a distinction has to be drawn between the number of mothers confined in a particular period, usually referred to as the number of maternities[1] and the total resultant births, live and still. In England and Wales in 1965 the ratio of births to maternities was 1011 births to every 1000 mothers confined. The frequencies of occurrence of different degrees of multiplicity were, in England and Wales, in 1965:

Type of multiple maternity	Frequency per 1,000 maternities
Twins	11·2
Triplets	0·091
Quadruplets	Nil
Quintuplets	Nil

[1] Strictly a maternity is defined in England and Wales as a pregnancy which has terminated in the birth of one or more live or stillborn child(ren).

VARIATION OF FERTILITY WITH AGE OF MOTHER
AND DURATION OF MARRIAGE

We may calculate age-marriage-duration specific fertility rates by classifying both maternities in the period and the average married female population in the period according to age of mother and duration of marriage and dividing the number of maternities for a particular age of mother and duration by the appropriate number of women at risk. In general, these fertility rates decline with advancing age of mother and with lengthening duration of marriage. At each duration the rates decline with increasing age of mother, and at each age of mother, after rising to a maximum in the second year of marriage (except in those under age 20 where pre-marital conceptions are relatively more numerous) they decline with lengthening duration of marriage.

These two factors of age and marriage duration are of considerable importance in assessing fertility prospects for a particular population.

Other Indices of Fertility

The birth rate in a particular year is merely a short term measure of the flow of births and gives no guidance to the long term effects of contemporary variations in fertility. The important fact to be ascertained is whether or not the current level of fertility, if maintained, is such that in the long run the population will change in size and age structure. From this problem there emerges the concept of population maintenance or replacement.

It might be thought that the natural increase was itself an adequate measure of population maintenance. The natural increase, however, though a correct arithmetical expression of the balance of births over total deaths, indicates only the population changes (aside from migration) in *one* year and not the trend. In any one year the total deaths depend upon the present age structure of the population which though affected by past fertility is not sensitive to current changes in fertility. If as in England past fluctuations in fertility and mortality have been such that a bulge in the curve of age distribution is working its way up through age groups (see p. 2) there will come a time when a large increase in the population at advanced ages will produce a sharp rise in the annual deaths. Thus it may be that even though fertility at that time may be rising the natural increase will be more affected by the change in the number of deaths than by changes in the flow of births. The two components of the natural increase are quite unrelated to each other and their coincidental balance though important cannot be expected to give any indication of the long term growth of the population.

The concept of replacement involves measurement of effects over a period of time and requires the focus of attention upon generations rather than on the addition of births within a short period of time.

Replacement

Suppose we consider the simplest measure of population maintenance. Assume that the current annual number of births continues indefinitely and calculate (using life table factors based on current mortality rates) the size of population that would ultimately result when stationary conditions had been attained. In England and Wales in 1961–5 the average annual number of live births was 848,554 and the deaths averaged 553,274. A population recruited from this supply of births and exposed to current mortality[1] would number 58·47 millions. The actual average population in the same period was 47·02 millions. Thus the number of births in 1961–5 though fifty-three per cent greater than the number of deaths in the period was only twenty-four per cent more than that (682,400) required to maintain the population.

It has, however, to be borne in mind that a large proportion of the population are not in the child-producing age group and therefore the current births can hardly be related to them. If in fact the important proportion within the child-bearing age group is temporarily unduly high, the births will be high in relation to the total population and the percentage maintenance of the current population *of all ages* will give too optimistic a picture. We shall have no warning that when the temporary inflation of the child-bearing age group passes, the flow of births may not suffice to maintain the population. We might, therefore, consider whether or not parents are maintaining the population of parents, calculated in exactly the same way as before except for the restriction of age.

Suppose we take the child-producing age group as 15–49. The 1961–5 births (848,554 average per annum) would maintain a stationary population containing 27·85 million persons (both sexes combined) aged 15–49. The actual population in England and Wales in the age groups numbered 21·82 million in 1961–5 (average). The extent of 'parental maintenance' as a percentage of 21·82 million was 128. It would in fact have required 665,000 births a year for parental replacement compared with 682,400 required on the total population basis used above. Thus, owing to the 1961–5 age structure of the population (with a low proportion in the parental age group) the number of births required to produce *parental* replacement would

[1] We multiply the male and female births by the life table factor T_x/l_0 for males and females respectively. Note that $T_x/l_0 = \overset{\circ}{e}_x$.

be less than sufficient to support the *total* population of all ages, though at this time the difference is not great. (If we were to go back to 1936–40 we would find that annual births were three per cent above *total* replacement but nine per cent *below* parental replacement. There was then a high proportion in the parental age group.)

Gross Reproduction Rate

Although we have taken account of the child-bearing population as distinct from the total population we have not sub-divided this population according to age in order to take account of differential fertility at different ages within the group. It is necessary to do this in order to obtain a clearer picture of possible variations such as may arise from unusual features of the age structure of the population even within the child-bearing group. The first step is to calculate the fertility rate *at each age* of parents, that is the ratio of the births of mothers (or fathers) of a particular age to the number of mothers (or fathers) living at that age.

With age fertility rates available we may now consider whether, if these rates are maintained, the mothers (or fathers) will produce sufficient girl infants (or boy infants) during the reproductive part of their lives (assumed to be 15–49) to replace themselves before they pass out of the parental age group. If mortality is ignored we add together the age fertility rates (for births of a particular sex) to yield the expected number of girls (boys) produced by women (men) in their reproductive lives. This is known as the gross reproduction rate, and a value of unity might be held to indicate 'replacement' (though we shall see later that this is not valid).

The calculation proceeds as follows (for women):

England and Wales—1965

Age	Female population (1,000)	Total live births (females only)	Mean fertility rate
15–19	1,822	39,408	0·02163
20–24	1,583	135,579	0·08565
25–29	1,479	128,098	0·08661
30–34	1,425	70,333	0·04936
35–39	1,488	35,185	0·02365
40–44	1,661	10,157	0·00611
45–49	1,477	684[1]	0·00046
Total	10,935	419,444	0·27347

[1] Including one birth to a mother aged 51.

It may be assumed that the mean fertility rate can be applied at individual years of age so that the sum of the age rates over the period 15–19 will be five times the mean rate (since five individual years of age are involved). Thus the total fertility (i.e. total expected births to a woman passing through the age group 15–49) = 5 × 0·27347 or 1·367. (Note that the total fertility rate is (for female births), 419,444/10,935,000 or 0·0384) and that applying this at all ages would give a crude index of 0·0384 × 35 or 1·344.

The gross reproduction rate may be expressed symbolically by the formula

$$\sum_{x=0}^{x=w} {}^s i_x$$

where ${}^s i_x$ = fertility rate at age x, specific for sex, i.e. female births to females or male births to males and w is the upper limit of reproductive age.

Net Reproduction Rate

The gross reproduction rate fails to take account of the mortality of infants before they themselves become the same age as that of the parents they are supposed to replace and of mortality among parents before the end of the child-bearing period. In order to make allowance for the mortality of infants we need to apply to the estimated births in each age group, survivorship factors up to the present age of the parent. The formula becomes

$$\sum_{0}^{w} {}^s i_x \cdot {}_x p_0$$

where ${}_x p_0$ is the chance of survival from birth to age x according to the currently applicable life table for the appropriate sex. The calculation proceeds as follows:

England and Wales—1965

Age group (1)	Fertility rate (female births) (2)	Survival factor (3)	(2) × (3) (4)
15–19	0·02163	0·9647	0·02087
20–24	0·08565	0·9609	0·08230
25–29	0·08661	0·9559	0·08279
30–34	0·04936	0·9500	0·04689
35–39	0·02365	0·9425	0·02229
40–44	0·00611	0·9321	0·00570
45–49	0·00046	0·9168	0·00042
Total			0·26126

Female net reproduction rate = 5 × 0·2613 or 1·306.

If the rate is greater than unity it is assumed that the population is more than maintaining or 'reproducing' itself.

It is important to bear in mind that for replacement to be attained a generation of women (or of men) must produce a replacement for every member of the generation. Thus the surviving adults of a generation must *on average* produce rather more than one replacement each, to allow for the fact that some children will fail to survive to adult life. Similarly a cohort of married couples must produce *on average* more than two children, since they must count on a double loss, namely, from death and from failure to marry. These generations or cohorts may replace themselves at any time during the thirty years or so of female reproductive life. It does not matter very much in which years they produce their children and any one year is a small fraction of the total thirty years. Furthermore, the total birth experience of a single calendar year consists of the aggregate of the experiences of a number of generations or alternatively of a number of marriage cohorts (i.e. women married in the same year). If each generation or cohort concerned has but few children in that year for some reason as economic depression or danger from war or wartime separation, nothing could be more ridiculous than to hypothesize that some future generation will, at each age, have the same low rates as those of the many generations concerned in the fertility of the particular year in question. The average addition to a family in a single year is thus a small part of the whole average family and calendar year reproduction rates (in any shape or form) are very imperfect measures of replacement. They are in fact nothing more than standardized calendar year birth rates on a scale which approaches unity at a replacement level. The value for a single year has no more significance than any other birth rate and only a persistent trend substantially above (below) unity might be an indication of a growing (declining) population.

Other Factors

The net reproduction rate makes allowance only for abnormal age distribution and mortality. Other factors need to be considered. A sudden rise in the marriage rate would produce temporary increases in age fertility rates in subsequent years. For this reason reproduction rates are sometimes marriage-standardized, though this raises the problem of choice of marriage basis, and the index is no longer automatic. It must be reiterated that family building suffers temporary fluctuations too, for example, when war or economic crises cause postponement of births which are later made up by equally temporary high fertility. As we have remarked this last type of variation may only be a change in the timing of births within the individual families without affecting the ultimate size of the families when completed. Fertility rates in such a period would not reflect the current trend of size of family in the population.

Cohort or Generation Analysis

Sharp changes in duration fertility rates may arise from changes in the timing of family building within married life without necessarily implying any change in the ultimate size of family. It is not therefore surprising that the average size of family of completed fertility (number of live born children produced by a married woman by the end of her reproductive period of life) has been found to exhibit much more stability than do the specific fertility rates from year to year. As the estimation of completed family size of married couples (as a means of estimating replacement prospects) is in fact the primary object of fertility studies modern demography has turned its attention to this measure.

Statistically this involves following through a group of persons born in a particular year (a generation) or married in a particular year (usually called a marriage cohort) throughout their lifetimes and recording the number of children they produce.

Considering first the marriage cohort we can see that the women who contribute to the fertility rate for marriage duration 0— in 1961, will contribute to the fertility rate for marriage duration 1— in 1962, 2— in 1963 and so on. The cumulation of these rates for all durations will produce the ultimate or completed family size of women married within the same period. In this example, however, the period will overlap calendar years as the births at duration 0— in 1961 will include those of women married in 1960 as well as those married early in 1961. It is usually desirable to follow a group of women married in a particular calendar year. For this reason it is necessary to tabulate the births not only by year of marriage duration but also by calendar year of marriage. The tabulation is also carried out separately for different age groups at marriage as the marriage age has an important effect on the family size—women married for the first time at age forty-five, for example, will already be near the end of their reproductive life and will have no opportunity to produce a large family. The cohort is then specified by age at marriage and (usually) calendar year of marriage.

Generation Replacement Rates

For considering the extent to which the population is replacing itself the marriage cohort experience is not very satisfactory, mainly because it is necessary to make some allowance for the number of female offspring who do not marry and are therefore not going to contribute to the replacement of the cohort (apart from the general allowance for illegitimate fertility). Their numbers can hardly be assessed from the marriage experience of the year in question for we are concerned with making some allowance for those only then born who will reach the end of their reproductive period without being married. For this the marriage experience of a single and current year may be a misleading guide; for example, economic conditions may later produce some temporary postponement of marriages or general reduction in marriage prospects. Nevertheless we can only use current nuptiality based on a period of years to assess the proportion of female births who will marry *and* survive the reproductive age period as in the following example:

England and Wales—Marriages of 1945

Age at marriage	Number of spinster marriages (thousands)	Projected ultimate family size (a)	Combined chance of surviving and of marrying between age 15 and 45 (b)
Under 20	56·9	2·75	
20–24	191·2	2·25	
25–29	66·3	1·90	
30–34	23·4	1·40	
35–39	11·1	0·73	
40–44	5·8	0·26	
	354·7	Mean 2·129	0·8689

Replacement Index (assuming female births 0·4854 of all births):

Legitimate (2·129 × 0·8689 × 0·4854)	0·898
Illegitimate (add 4·7 per cent)	0·042
	0·940

(a) By simple extrapolation of family size (live born children) as shown for successive years of marriage duration year by year in Table PP of the Registrar General's Statistical Review Part II.

(b) According to a joint mortality and nuptiality table (with allowance for risk of marriage being broken before age 45). Strictly this factor should be varied according to the period of time over which the family is produced to allow for generation changes in mortality and marriage rates, but this has been ignored for simplicity.

The calculation is not entirely satisfactory because it involves a mixture of generations with differing marriage and mortality prospects. It seems preferable therefore to abandon year of marriage as the reference point in favour of year of birth, i.e. to calculate a replacement rate applicable to a single generation—those born in a particular calendar year. For this purpose we follow the generation throughout childhood marriage and reproductive life subjecting to it the mortality, nuptiality and fertility actually recorded for that generation if it has reached the end of reproductive life, or forecast for it if not.

The computation if performed correctly is complicated and laborious but not essentially difficult. The stages are as follows:

(a) A combined mortality and nuptiality table is constructed which shows at age x the number of women surviving to that age from 100,000 births (or some other convenient starting number, or radix as it is called), and among these the distribution by marital status. The table would also show the number of spinster marriages, widowhoods, divorces, remarriages and deaths, based on the rates of decrement assumed in the table. The married women of age x are divided according to the duration of their current marriage.

(b) At each age and marriage duration the specific legitimate fertility rate appropriate to the age and duration and to the class of married woman (once married or re-married) is applied to estimate the number of live births for that interval. At each age illegitimate fertility rates are applied to the unmarried women. The addition of these births when divided by the original radix of the nuptiality and mortality table gives the average family size for the generation. Application of the ratio of female to male births yields the number of female births to replace each original female birth, viz. the generation replacement rate.

A close approximation to the rate may be obtained by using a procedure similar to that outlined above for the marriage cohort. The difference is that in the column headed 'number of spinster marriages' the actual numbers of marriages of the cohort are replaced by the numbers relating to a particular generation (derived from an abridged nuptiality table). As we are dealing with the marriage experience of the whole generation, there is no longer any need for the factor 0·8689 in the above example which allowed for replacement of unmarried females (this factor will be implicit in the relationship between the size of the generation (the radix of the nuptiality table) and the total number of marriages up to the end of the reproductive period). Otherwise the calculation follows the same procedure.

Differential Fertility

Fertility varies not only with age and duration of marriage but also with occupation and social class, area of residence (for example, rural or urban), religion and many other factors. These factors are clearly of interest to those who may have to estimate the possible effect of steps taken by the community to influence fertility through any of them, for example, family allowances, or of social changes, for example, urbanization.

Features which have to be borne in mind are heterogeneity of occupational classes, differing average age of marriage (professional men may defer marriage until attainment of a certain status), changes in occupation between the ages of highest fertility and those at which the fertility is recorded.

Studies of differential fertility associated with the population censuses in England and Wales indicate that generally the lower social classes have always had, and continue to have, larger families than the higher social classes. The social gradient is becoming less pronounced and the underlying influences and attitudes tend to be different as fertility becomes more widely under voluntary control. Groups with the largest mean family size and smallest proportion childless are the manual workers, especially the unskilled and semi-skilled, members of the armed forces (other ranks) and farmers and agricultural workers. At the other end of the scale there are the clerical workers, managerial and professional workers, traders and shop assistants. Fertility also varies inversely with length of full-time education.

To deal properly with social and economic differentials in fertility would require a book in itself. So far as *methods* are concerned there are no new points. The need for a high degree of specificity in the statistical indices used, should be stressed. This involves classifying births and populations by age, year of birth, occupation, industry, education, urban/rural and religion. Adequate amounts of data to sustain such a refined analysis are normally only available from a population census. Religion is however not recorded at censuses in England and Wales and for measurement of this factor an *ad hoc* survey would be required.

REFERENCES

Fertility of Marriage, Census of England and Wales 1911. General Register Office (1917).

Fertility Report, Census of England and Wales 1951. General Register Office (1958).

Fertility Tables, Census of England and Wales 1961. General Register Office (1966).

Kiser, C. V. (ed.) *Research in Family Planning*. Princeton University Press (1962).

Meade, J. E. and Parkes, Λ. S. (ed.) *Genetic and Environmental Factors in Human Ability*. Oliver and Boyd, London (1966).

Glass, D. V. and Grebenik, E. 'The Trend and Pattern of Fertility in Great Britain', *Report on the Royal Commission on Population*. H.M.S.O. (1954).

Proceedings of the World Population Conference 1965, Volume II, United Nations (1967). (This volume contains papers reviewing fertility changes in many different countries.)

6

Marriage rates

As for all other vital rates, marriages must be related to the population at risk, viz. first marriages of females to the spinster population; remarriages to the numbers of widowed or divorced. The likelihood of marriage varies very much with the age of the prospective bride (or bridegroom).

It is usual therefore to calculate age specific marriage rates as in the example below.

TABLE FIVE

England and Wales 1965

Annual marriage rates per 1,000 bachelors, widowers and divorced men, spinsters, widows and divorced women by age

Age	Bachelors	Widowers and divorced men	Spinsters	Widows and divorced women
15–19	15·5	—	61·4	—
20–24	161·5	808·1	259·5	481·4
25–29	185·3	507·1	153·7	342·0
30–34	84·7	350·6	70·8	218·0
35–39	45·5⎫	190·3	39·1⎫	93·7
40–44	24·8⎭		22·0⎭	
45–49	16·6⎫	96·6	13·7⎫	30·4
50–54	10·4⎭		8·2⎭	
55 and over	4·2	21·3	2·2	3·2

THE BALANCE OF THE SEXES

The likelihood of marriage also depends on the relative supply of bachelors and spinsters. As an illustration we may look at changes in this country in recent times. In the early thirties as a result of a consistent stream of emigration of men from this country and the heavy losses of men in World War I there were in England and Wales more spinsters than was necessary to meet the bachelor demand. After the economic depression of the thirties the flow of emigrants was reversed, and has never been resumed on the same scale. The

war losses of 1939–45 were much lower than those of the period
1914–18. Furthermore the progressive reduction of foetal mortality
has resulted in a higher male/female ratio at birth. The reduction of
mortality at younger ages too has narrowed the mortality differential
between the two sexes and postponed the age group in which the
excess of males at birth is countered by excess male mortality from
5–9 in 1911 to 30–34 in 1961. All in all, the spinster excess of former
years has disappeared. We may demonstrate the change in the following way. In considering the relative supply of unmarried men and
women we must first make an allowance for the difference in age at
marriage. A rough allowance can be made by relating the average
of the male populations at ages 15–44 and 20–44 last birthday
(about $17\frac{1}{2}$–45 in exact years) to the average of the female populations
at ages 15–44 and 15–39 last birthday (15–$42\frac{1}{2}$ in exact years). The
ratios (males/females per 1,000) are:

	Census						
	1871	*1901*	*1911*	*1921*	*1931*	*1951*	*1961*
All conditions	877	876	892	846	892	988	1,000
Unmarried	786	787	808	724	800	968	1,059

(per thousand)

These figures show clearly the approach toward a balance between
the sexes.

ECONOMIC AND SOCIAL FACTORS AFFECTING
MARRIAGE RATES

An atmosphere of economic security encourages high marriage
rates. Recent conditions of full employment in England and Wales
have operated in two ways. First, employers have been competing
for labour and have had to offer, at the outset, rates of pay much
nearer to full adult rates than were formerly regarded as appropriate.
Secondly, jobs are not so eagerly sought after that spinsters have to
make way on marriage for unmarried women. It is now possible
and indeed regarded as desirable for women to follow a career
without having it cut short by marriage; or to put it the other way
round, to be able to contemplate marriage against a background of
joint earnings and a high level of living from the outset. Marriage
need not, as was formerly the case, be deferred until savings have
been acquired to furnish a home and provide a bulwark against any
risk of economic troubles in the early years of marriage. There is no
longer any economic obstacle to early marriage. Another factor to
be mentioned is the general emancipation of women. Marriage is
no longer regarded as the only 'safe' career for a girl. Socially, as
well as economically, girls can regard marriage as incidental to their

TABLE SIX

A net nuptiality table

x	Number of spinsters living at exact age x	Central rates of death dm_x	Central rates of first marriage mm_x	Probability of death or marriage $\dfrac{2(dm_x + mm_x)}{2 + (dm_x + mm_x)}$	Deaths x to x+1	Marriages x to x+1
0	10,000					
15	9,661[1]	0·00052	—	0·00052	5	—
16	9,656	0·00058	0·00657	0·00712	6	63
17	9,587	0·00064	0·02599	0·02628	6	246
etc.						

[1] By ordinary life table processes (as in the line for age 15). For age 17 we have, total decrement = 9,587 × 0·02628 = 252 of which deaths = mean population × central death rate = [9,587 − ½(252)] × 0·00064 = 6 and marriages = 252 − 6 = 246. A central rate is the average rate over the age interval, e.g. a central marriage rate at age 17 is obtained by dividing the number of marriages at age 17 last birthday in a specified period by the mean population at that age during the same period.

fuller lives. Girls do not regard themselves as waiting to be 'married off' after a respectable period of courtship.

As a result of all these factors, in England and Wales as in many other countries the period since World War II has been characterized by high marriage rates and earlier marriage ages. As already indicated in Chapter 2, one way of summarizing a set of marriage rates is to produce a table showing, out of a given generation of female births, the proportion still alive and (a) unmarried or (b) married, at any particular age. Such a table is derived from a combination of marriage rates and mortality rates and is called a 'net nuptiality table'. The term 'net' indicates that mortality has been taken into account as well as nuptiality. If marriages only were considered it would be a gross nuptiality table. The latter type of table is rarely used.

The probabilities of marriage on which the abridged nuptiality tables for a given year are based refer to the experience of different generations for a single calendar year. One effect of this is to make them of limited value as a guide to long-term prospects. For this purpose it would be better to compare the experiences of different generations at the same ages but in different calendar periods, rather than different generations at different ages in the same calendar period.

Table Seven illustrates the process. This is obtained by relating the proportion married at age x in calendar year y, to year of birth $y - x$. The proportion 854 shown for women of ages 30–34 for years of birth 1917–21 represents the average proportion for that age group in a period of ten years centred at 1951. The actual proportion for 1951 has been taken as an approximation to this value to save arithmetic. In earlier years these proportions were available only in census years and therefore some interpolation has been necessary.

TOTAL MARRIED WOMEN OF REPRODUCTIVE AGE

The effect of high marriage rates in raising the proportion of the population which is married is an important influence on the fertility of the community since this depends on the number of married women in the population.

The proportion married increases with advancing age, at first rapidly and then more slowly, and then begins to decline as new marriages are increasingly offset by widowhood. In England and Wales the proportion married has increased within each age group throughout the current century.

The proportion married in the 15–49 age group represents the fraction of the reproductive years which fall within married life.

TABLE SEVEN

Proportions ever married among generations of men and women born since 1862, England and Wales (per thousand)

Age of men							Period of Birth	Age of women					
15–	20–	25–	30–	35–	40–	45–49		15–	20–	25–	30–	35–	40–	45–49
5	209[1]	573	751[1]	824	855[1]	873	1862-66	26	318[1]	606	749[1]	801	824[1]	835
4	184[1]	548	735[1]	814	855[1]	876	1872-76	20	286[1]	588	736[1]	790	820[1]	832
3	155[1]	508	746[1]	837	876[1]	890	1882-86	16	255[1]	566	733[1]	796	820[1]	832
2	161[1]	554	777[1]	863	889[1]	906	1892-96	12	258[1]	590	744[1]	794	821[1]	831
4	160[1]	529	763	864	881	902	1902-06	18	257	594	740	801	836	848
3	139	530	803	864	891	911	1907-11	14	258	616	783	832	858	869
3	152	617	798	867	897	905	1912-16	18	290	719	829	867	895	895
6	203	612	810	875	893	—	1917-21	22	402	713	854	890	903	—
9	199	651	835	868	—	—	1922-26	39	442	783	884	902	—	—
9	238	665	825	—	—	—	1927-31	35	482	813	891	—	—	—
5	277	706	—	—	—	—	1932-36	44	542	843	—	—	—	—
8	310	—	—	—	—	—	1937-41	55	580	—	—	—	—	—
11	—	—	—	—	—	—	1942-46	66	—	—	—	—	—	—

[1] Interpolated values

There was a slight increase in this fraction from 50·2 per cent to 52·9 per cent between 1911 and 1931 followed by a more rapid rise to 56·6 per cent in 1938 and 70·1 per cent in 1961. These increases are partly due to the ageing of the 15–49 age group since 1911 which has increased the relative number at the older ages in this age group where the proportion married is greater. This element can be removed by calculating the number of women who would have been married if the individual age group proportions married had been those of 1911; the actual number of married women can then be divided by the standardized number to produce a set of marriage indices standardized on the 1911 proportions married. These indices are compared with the unstandardized figures in the following statement:

Year	1911	1921	1931	1941	1951	1961
Standardized	1·000	1·008	1·022	1·125	1·200	1·298
Unstandardized	1·000	1·025	1·054	1·201	1·327	1·396

The above figures show that the true increase since 1911 in the proportion married among women aged 15–49 was thirty per cent compared with the forty per cent suggested by the unstandardized proportions. A quarter of the latter increase is due to the ageing of the population and is unrelated to the changing incidence of marriage.

Other Fertility Effects

Apart from adding to the flow of births generally by increasing the stock of married women, the rise in marriage rates has had an accelerating effect on the flow of births in so far as this rise in marriage incidence has been concentrated at young ages and has helped, together with faster family building within marriage, to depress the average age at parenthood. This means, shortly, borrowing births from the future to augment temporarily the normal flow. It has been estimated that of the rise in annual births between 1955 and 1960 in England and Wales about one-quarter was due to earlier marriage and a higher proportion marrying, and about three-quarters to shortening of the average interval between marriage and first birth and between subsequent births. There has been little sign of any substantial rise in average family size. Any permanent effect upon fertility has been reduced by the growing tendency (common to most communities where family limitation is practised) for family building to be completed relatively early in married life and not to be proportionally extended by any increase in the length of married life falling within the reproductive age period. In a developing country without family planning fertility would probably rise with an extension of married life within the reproductive age period.

Employment of Married Women

The changes in marriage rates are connected with the employment of married women in two ways. The rise in marriage rates has been encouraged by the extensive employment of married women; this extensive employment has become essential owing to the decline in the size of the spinster population available for employment. We are approaching in England and Wales a pattern of early marriage and child-bearing with, as soon as is practicable, a return to the adopted vocational career—provided that the job is not less interesting than staying at home.

Summary

With numbers of bachelors and spinsters more in balance and against a background of full employment (including continued employment in marriage) marriage rates have risen—and average age at marriage has fallen. There has been a real decline in spinsterhood. In England and Wales current marriage rates imply that 95 per cent of spinsters will marry before the age of 50. This proportion is about as high as is possible when it is borne in mind that a small proportion of women (and men) will always be physically and psychologically unsuited for marriage. Though we have used recent changes in England and Wales to illustrate methodology, the methodology itself is of general application.

Marital condition is an important factor in relation to mortality and employment but obviously from a demographic point of view the level and future course of marriage rates are most important in relation to their influence on fertility. Indeed it is impossible to separate fertility rates from the age and marriage duration structure of the population of married women supporting these rates. Fertility rates must always be considered against the marriage experience permitting them.

In general, higher marriage rates, especially at younger ages, tend to higher fertility simply because more married women are exposed to the risk of conception for longer. When we came to discuss fertility measurement it was seen that the number of married women at a particular age entered into the calculation of reproduction and replacement rates.

REFERENCES

Benjamin, B. 'Changes in Marriage Incidence in Western Society in the last Thirty Years', *Journal of the Institute of Actuaries* 89, 125–34 (1963).

Hajnal, J. *European Marriage Patterns in Perspective*, in "*Population in History.*" Arnold, London (1965).

Proceedings of the World Population Conference 1965, Volume II (the reference to marriage as a factor in fertility). United Nations (1967).

7

Mortality measurement

Death Rates

The purpose of measuring mortality is to enable inferences to be drawn about the likelihood of deaths occurring within a specific population during a specified period of time. It is natural therefore for the basic measure to be expressed in proportional terms as a rate of mortality—the number of deaths occurring per unit of population in a particular interval of time. The unit of population may commonly be 1,000, 10,000,100,000 or one million; it is a matter of arithmetical convenience. For example the vital statistician may express 2,564 deaths in a general population of 216,342 persons in a year as an annual death rate of 1,185 deaths per 100,000 or 12 per 1,000 according to the number of significant figures he wishes to record. It is necessary to define not only the interval of time and the unit of population size but also to define what kind of deaths (all or those from a particular cause) and what kind of population (the general population or those in a particular sex, age, etc., category).

The reason for this is that the risk of dying varies with a number of factors—sex and age and other factors—which either influence the physical constitution or the environment of the people, such as birthplace, geographical locality of residence, occupation, marital condition. In calculating rates of mortality it is therefore necessary to differentiate the influence of these factors as well as to distinguish the contribution of different medical causes of death (types of disease or injury). Death rates may therefore be classified as general or specific, the first relating to all causes of death and to the general population, the second to special causes of death or to deaths in particular sections of the population, or both. In the latter event the extent of specificity must be carefully defined, for example the death rate from pneumonia among married males aged 40–44, last birthday, in England and Wales during 1966.

Whether general or specific death rates are under consideration it is important to be sure that the population used in the calculation is precisely that which produced the deaths also used in the calculation; conversely the deaths must comprise all those occurring in this population and no others. The denominator of the rate (of which the numerator is the relevant number of deaths) is commonly referred to as 'the population at risk' or the 'exposed to risk'. In the example given above we should have, in the numerator of the rate, every death in 1966 of a married man aged 40–44 at death resident in England and Wales certified as due to penumonia as the underlying cause; in the denominator every married man aged 40–44 resident in England and Wales during 1966. This immediately raises the question of what we mean by 'during 1966'.

The population at risk in most vital statistical calculations is the mean population of the area (or class of person considered) over the period to which the rate relates. It will be seen later that this kind of death rate is not the same concept as the age specific rate of mortality used in life table calculations—though except where mortality is changing rapidly with age it is not numerically very different. As a first approximation the mid-year (or mid-interval) population is accepted as the mean unless irregular or rapid changes in the population (as, for example, during a war) render it necessary to make more precise calculations of the average number actually at risk. Death rates when calculated for a shorter period than a year are often expressed as an equivalent *annual* rate, viz. as the annual rate that would result from the persistence of the same mortality conditions for a full year.

This conversion is merely for convenience since it is often confusing to pass from annual to quarterly rates and therefore desirable to work with rates of the same order of size throughout. The conversion though convenient may often be unrealistic. To assume that the mortality of a particular quarter which includes a widespread epidemic of influenza, could persist for a whole year would not be justifiable but it is usually accepted that conversion is made without such implication. The shorter the interval the more likely it is that the rate will be influenced by some epidemic occurrence or a spell of particularly inclement weather so that while the rate for a very short period is a fact and a true statement of mortality for that period, extreme care should be exercised not to draw inferences about mortality at other times or over longer intervals.

It should also be borne in mind that where small numbers of deaths are involved, chance fluctuations are likely to be relatively large. For example, suppose we have a population of only 1,000 with over a long period of years an average death rate of 13 per 1,000 per year. This means an average annual number of deaths of

13; but any elementary statistical textbook will tell us that the frequency distribution of the annual deaths will be such that fluctuations to fewer than six or to more than twenty will occur in each case as often as once in forty years and that although the long run average will be thirteen, in any one year it is likely as not that the number of deaths will be *outside* the range 11–15. Looking at the

TABLE EIGHT

England and Wales, 1965
rates of mortality per 1,000

Age group	Males	Females
0–	21·48	16·39
1–4	0·87	0·76
5–9	0·48	0·31
10–14	0·42	0·29
15–19	1·00	0·40
20–24	1·05	0·45
25–34	1·07	0·68
35–44	2·48	1·79
45–54	7·36	4·36
55–64	21·4	10·3
65–74	53·0	28·3
75–84	118·4	79·2
85 and over	242·4	197·1

problem the other way round we can see that a particular year when there was a chance occurrence of say eighteen deaths would be a very misleading basis for calculating the underlying mortality. Where populations or rates are small it is advisable to base calculations upon a group of years rather than upon a single year in order to increase the number of deaths involved and thus to reduce the size of the possible error.

Variation of Mortality with Age and Sex

Mortality is highest at the extremes of age (see Table Eight). Once the newborn infant has survived the hazards of the first few days of life mortality falls rapidly and during childhood the risk is very small. In adolescence the impact and strain of industrial life brings a rise in mortality. These and other factors, inherent in the social and economic environment and individual ways of life, lead to a continuing increase in the risk of death as age advances. At later ages the wearing out of the human frame rather than inimical qualities of the environment becomes the dominant cause of mortality.

The death rates for females are lower than those for males at all ages. Briefly, the higher mortality of males may be explained in medical terms as follows:

(*a*) In infancy and early childhood, boys are generally more vulnerable to some birth hazards (prematurity, malformation, birth injury), to infection, possibly as a result of some biological factor, and to injuries, possibly as a result of more vigorous and venturesome activity; these being the principal causes of death at these ages.

(*b*) In early and middle adult life the principal causes of death are accidents and violence, tuberculosis, heart disease and cancer and except for the latter cause the death rates are higher in men. The excessive mortality from tuberculosis in men (except in very early adult life) is part of the generally greater vulnerability of men to respiratory disease of all kinds, not only tuberculosis but also bronchitis, influenza, pneumonia, cancer of the lung (and this greater vulnerability extends to advanced ages). The type of heart disease which is most responsible for deaths in this age group is arterial and described as coronary thrombosis—there is still considerable controversy as to the factors operating to increase susceptibility to this disease. An excessive diet, insufficient physical activity and nervous tension, seem to play their part, and sedentary occupations appear to incur, for these or other reasons, a higher risk. The higher risk of accidents must be regarded as occupational in the broader sense of including, as compared with females, more outdoor movement in traffic, etc., as well as greater industrial hazards.

(*c*) At more advanced ages the process of physical deterioration and lessening resistance to disease associated with general wear and tear appear to proceed faster in men. Age for age cerebral haemorrhages, arterial disease, cancer (especially of the lung) and bronchitis take a heavier toll of males than females.

Enough is already known of the natural history of diseases and the social and environmental factors in their aetiology to render profitable the study of death rates specific, not only for age and sex, but also for cause—as certified by the medical practitioner in attendance prior to death, or by the coroner in cases necessitating inquest. The study of such rates over periods of time and in different areas may help to indicate the relative weight of various occupational and environmental factors in the different areas and the relative progress made in those areas toward reducing mortality.

Finally there are ethnic factors to be taken into account. In the United States of America the mortality of the white population is considerably lighter than among the non-white at all except the extremely advanced ages. To what extent this difference is of truly racial origin or merely reflects different social and economic conditions is not clear but certainly the statistical separation is important. In England and Wales there are as yet insufficient coloured people to render necessary the preparation of separate statistics but there is growing interest in health problems associated with large-scale immigration.

Mortality Indices

In 1961 the crude death rate in Bournemouth was 13·2 per 1,000 living and the corresponding rate for Corby was only 5·2. These two figures do not indicate the real difference in the mortality risks of the populations of the two towns at that time. Bournemouth is a coastal town attractive to older retired persons—in 1961 twenty-two per cent of the population was aged sixty-five or more—and this means the population is abnormal by virtue of a shortage of young persons. The effect on the death rate is to reduce the denominator without proportionately reducing the numerator (because young people do not contribute many deaths) and thus to inflate the rate. On the other hand Corby is a new and rapidly developing town growing up round an expanding steel works; many young families have moved there and in consequence the population is short of old persons. This affects the numerator more than the denominator and deflates the crude mortality rate.

Consider the following example:

Age	Area A			Area B		
	Population	Deaths	Death rate per 1,000	Population	Deaths	Death rate per 1,000
	(thousands)			(thousands)		
0–4	280	1,400	5·00	220	2,200	10·00
5–24	900	900	1·00	810	1,215	1·50
25–44	910	2,730	3·00	900	2,970	3·30
45–64	720	14,400	20·00	780	11,700	15·00
65 and over	310	38,750	125·00	350	38,500	110·00
All ages	3,120	58·180	18·65	3,060	56,585	18·49

The crude death rates are 18·65 and 18·49 per 1,000 but their general similarity conceals the fact that the age specific rates in area B are higher at young ages and lower at older ages than in area A, i.e. the age incidence of mortality is very different. But the age structure of the population of B is so much older than that of A that it produces an elevation of the crude death rate to compensate for the lighter age specific mortality rates.

It must be borne in mind that the crude death rate is a weighted average of age specific rates in which the weights are the numbers of the population in the respective age groups, i.e. if $m_{x,t}$ is the death rate at ages x to $x + t$ and $E_{x,t}^c$ is the population in the same age group, the total deaths will be $\Sigma E_{x,t}^c \cdot m_{x,t}$ where the summation is over all age groups, and the total population $\Sigma E_{x,t}^c$ so that the crude death rate is

$$\frac{\Sigma E_{x,t}^c \cdot m_{x,t}}{\Sigma E_{x,t}^c}$$

Clearly if the values of $E_{x,t}^c$ are increased for older ages at the expense of the younger ages then, nothwithstanding the constancy of the age rates of mortality, the crude death rate will rise. The weights used in such an average are therefore important. ($E_{x,t}^c$ is used to symbolize the central or average population exposed to risk.)

The Use of a Single Figure Index

Before taking this any further we should consider why it is that an average should be used at all. It ought to be evident that since mortality varies with age, and population age structure varies with area, then in comparing mortality in two different areas we ought to look at the individual age specific rates. However it is difficult mentally to assimilate a large number of rates and for many purposes (e.g. for brevity in description, ease in manipulation, etc.) it is desirable to have a summary measure to try to accomplish what the mind finds difficult to do unaided, i.e. to epitomize the whole experience. This is of course the fundamental object and justification of any type of average or index figure. It will be understood that this desire for a single measure or average is increased by virtue of the fact that mortality varies with many other characteristics such as sex, marital condition, ethnic origin and social conditions, etc., so that for really thorough comparisons one very large number of refined specific rates may be involved. It has to be said at once that no one average is accepted as sufficient for all purposes.

Standardization

We have seen that the crude death rate is one such average but that it suffers from the defect that the weights used in its calculation are the local age group populations, i.e. they vary from area to area.

Nevertheless this defect is not serious for the very large number of areas whose population have a structure of the same general character, and the crude death rate is indeed widely used in such circumstances. Where there is no precise knowledge of the population structure, i.e. where only the total deaths and the total population are known, there is of course no alternative to this procedure. Where the age structure is known however, i.e. where the age specific rates of mortality are known, there is no reason why in calculating the average death rate we should not avoid using weights which vary from area to area by deciding to use a fixed set of weights, i.e. a *standard* population structure. Such an average rate then becomes a *standardized mortality rate*. Since populations can vary in their sex proportions at each age it is usual to standardize rates for *persons* for this source of variation also.

Direct standardization

Employing the same notation as before but using the symbol $^sE^c$ to indicate the standard population and remembering that the rates are specific also for *sex* and the summation is over all ages (and, for persons rates, is performed for *the two sexes* separately);

$$\text{Standardized mortality rate} = \frac{\Sigma^s E^c_{x,t} \cdot m_{x,t}}{\Sigma^s E^c_{x,t}}$$

Indirect Standardization

Where for example, a large number of district rates of mortality require standardization on the basis of the national population, the direct method would entail a very large amount of computation; moreover age specific rates and age analysis of the population may not be available for the districts.

It would clearly be a simpler process if we could find a factor F such that, when the crude death rate of a district is multiplied by it, the result is equal to the standardized mortality rate, viz.:

$$\left[\frac{\Sigma E^c_{x,t} m_{x,t}}{\Sigma E^c_{x,t}}\right] \times F = \left[\frac{\Sigma^s E^c_{x,t} m_{x,t}}{\Sigma^s E^c_{x,t}}\right]$$

where the values of the bracketed expressions are known but not necessarily the individual elements in the summations.

To calculate F we use the specific death rates for the standard population in this equation instead of the district rates (which may not be known).

$$F = \left[\frac{\Sigma^s E^c_{x,t} \, ^s m_{x,t}}{\Sigma^s E^c_{x,t}}\right] \div \left[\frac{\Sigma E^c_{x,t} \, ^s m_{x,t}}{\Sigma E^c_{x,t}}\right]$$

i.e. if the district population were subject at each age to the same mortality as in the standard population its crude death rate would still be different from that of the standard population to the extent that the age structure of the district population differs from that of the standard population. If the district population is of an older age structure the crude rate will be inflated and F, to correct for this inflation, will be correspondingly less than unity, for example if the inflation is $33\frac{1}{3}$ per cent, F will be $100/133\frac{1}{3}$ or $0\cdot75$. F will only apply to similar degrees of distortion, i.e. to circumstances where the general pattern of mortality is similar to that of the standard population since we have assumed that the distortion is the same even though ${}^s m_{x,t}$ has been substituted for $m_{x,t}$, but it is usually valid to make this assumption. We still require $E_{x,t}^c$. These age group populations will be available at times of population census and except when violent population changes are taking place it may be possible to assume that they remain sufficiently stable to permit the use of F, once calculated, throughout the intercensal period and until the next census makes it possible to recalculate F.

In England and Wales, factors similar to F are used by the Registrar General to adjust local death rates to the national population structure (i.e. in this case the standard population death rates are the national rates for the current year) and these factors are then called *Area Comparability Factors*.

Choice of a Standard Population

Up to 1941 the Regstrar General of England and Wales published:

(a) Death rates for each sex standardized for age, and a death rate for persons standardized for sex and age, for all causes combined;

(b) for selected causes of death, age-standardized rates for males and females separately.

The standard population used was that of England and Wales in 1901. The direct method was employed. Specimen figures are given below.

It will be seen from these figures that owing to the ageing of the population from 1871 to 1940 the higher death rates at older ages received growing weight in the crude death rate which became more and more in excess of the average based upon a standard population. According to the crude persons rate mortality decreased over the period by forty-three per cent; but the standardized rate was reduced by fifty-four per cent.

It will be noticed that the standardized rate for 1931–40 is only 9·3 per 1,000 compared with a crude rate of 12·3. This is because the population of 1901 had a 'young' age structure (32·4 per cent at ages nought to fourteen and only 4·7 per cent at ages sixty-five and over) favouring a low aggregate mortality. Such rates (which were in effect abstract figures rather than crude rates actually experienced) could only be compared among themselves and would be too low

TABLE NINE

England and Wales—death rates 1871–1940

Period	Crude death rates per 1,000 living			Standardized rates per 1,000 living		
	Persons	Males	Females	Persons	Males	Females
1871–1880	21·4	22·7	20·1	20·3	21·8	19·0
1881–1890	19·1	20·3	18·1	18·6	20·0	17·3
1891–1900	18·2	19·3	17·1	18·1	19·5	16·7
1901–1910	15·4	16·4	14·4	15·2	16·6	13·9
1911–1920	14·4	15·9	13·0	13·5	15·0	12·2
1921–1930	12·1	12·9	11·4	10·6	11·8	9·5
1931–1940	12·3	13·1	11·5	9·3	10·6	8·2

for comparison with any other country where rates have not been reduced to the same or at least to a closely similar standard.

The fact that standardized rates are low or 'young' looking does not destroy their value for depicting the mortality trend freed of distortion due to changes in population. It is possible that the choice of standard population might affect the relative emphasis given to mortality at younger ages (where improvement has been greater) and so might affect to a small extent the degree of decline in aggregate mortality.

Nevertheless the General Register Office in 1938 took the view that the 1901 population was too youthful, and inappropriate to current conditions; it also thought that any fixed standard population then chosen would rapidly become out of accord with actual conditions. For these reasons it was decided to cease to standardize strictly. A new Comparative Mortality Index was introduced which represented the ratio of aggregate mortality in the year of observation to that of a base year (1938), on the basis of a population structure *intermediate* between the two years.

C.M.I. (year y) $= \Sigma m_y(P_y + P_{38}) \div \Sigma m_{38}(P_y + P_{38})$ where m_y and m_{38} were the sex-age death rates for years y and 1938 and P_y and P_{38} were the proportions within corresponding sex age groups of the total populations of the respective years.

Thus the C.M.I. was a ratio of death rates and did not have the characteristics of death rate itself. It was age adjusted in a manner which varied from year to year, offending to an increasing extent against the very principle of standardization. It has never been adopted by any other country.

In 1958 the C.M.I. was abandoned by the General Register Office in favour of the so called 'standardized mortality ratio'. This does not involve a standard population as such. It is a method familiar to actuaries—the comparison of actual deaths in a particular population with those which would be expected if 'standard' age specific rates applied, viz:

$$\frac{\Sigma E_x^c \cdot {}^s m_{x,t}}{\Sigma E_x^c \cdot m_{x,t}}$$

which can be written

$$\frac{\Sigma E_x^c \cdot m_{x,t} \left(\dfrac{{}^s m_{x,t}}{m_{x,t}} \right)}{\Sigma E_x^c \cdot m_{x,t}}$$

i.e. it is a weighted average of the age specific mortality differentials ($^s m/m$) where the weights are the actual deaths in each age group.

Other Standardized Measures

A single figure index which has sometimes been used is the 'life table death rate', i.e. the ratio of the number of deaths of persons above any defined age to the number living above that age in a stationary population (a population distributed on the basis of the 'living' column of the relevant life table). This is, of course, the reciprocal of the expectation of life. The expectation of life is itself a widely used single figure index of mortality (or rather of survival). The standardized death rate as calculated by the direct method can be expressed as a weighted mean of ratios of age rates with the deaths in the standard population age groups as the weights (see equation (2) below). Thus this is not independent of the standard population. The indirect method can also be criticized since the weights are not constant for all comparisons. An alternative is the 'equivalent average death rate', i.e. a rate standardized by reference to a population with equal numbers in the age groups. This is thus an arithmetic mean of the rates for age groups up to some convenient limit, such as sixty-five (beyond which it becomes unrealistic).

Yerushalmy (Am. J. Pub., 1950) referred to the difficulty that, in normal direct standardized comparison, the age rate ratios were weighted by the deaths in the standard population with the result that undue representation was given to mortality at old ages where deaths were heavy and secular improvement slight, while little account was taken of mortality at younger ages where deaths were few but improvement considerable. In order to give more representation to this important improvement at young ages he suggested weighting so that equal proportionate changes in age rates affect equally the mortality index (as the standardized rate now becomes) no matter at what ages these changes occur.

Starting with the normal expression for the standardized death rate we have:

$$\text{Standardized death rate} = \frac{\Sigma m_{x,t} \, {}^s E_{x,t}^c}{\Sigma {}^s E_{x,t}^c} \tag{1}$$

$$= \frac{1}{{}^s E^c} \Sigma \left(\frac{m_{x,t}}{{}^s m_{x,t}}\right) {}^s d_{x,t} \tag{2}$$

Where ${}^s d_{x,t}$ is the number of deaths in the standard population corresponding to ${}^s m_{x,t}$ and ${}^s E^c$ is the total standard population.

Yerushalmy effectively replaces ${}^s d_{x,t}$ by t, i.e. the age specific mortality differentials are given equal weights. Kohn (Can. J. Pub., 1951) has proposed that if there is to be prior assessment of the weight to be given to a particular age group in averaging improvement then there would be an advantage in separating the derivation of weights from the deaths or death rate of the age group for the disease involved, and in producing a system of weights which would be capable of universal application. Kohn suggests using the reciprocal of the age of death—in practice the reciprocal of the midpoint of the age interval of each age group, viz.:

$$\text{mortality index} = \frac{\Sigma m_{x,t} \cdot (t/a)}{\Sigma(t/a)}$$

where t = class interval
     a = age at midpoint.

This however removes any reference to comparison with standard mortality and is a different kind of average from those considered above.

We may now summarize the various systems of weights in weighted averages of the age mortality rate ratios ($m_{x,t}/{}^s m_{x,t}$).

Index	Weights
Standardized—direct	Actual *deaths* in age group in standard population
—indirect	Approximation to above
Standardized mortality ratio	Actual *deaths* in age group in actual population[1]
Yerushalmy	Equal

Infant Mortality

There has been no index of mortality more frequently used than the infant mortality rate—deaths of infants under one year of age per 1,000 live births. Most of the deaths after the first days are due to exogenous causes—mainly infections—and until recent times, when this component has shrunk to very small proportions, the rate was a sensitive index of social conditions, and of public health progress. Like the expectation of life it has the attraction of being a single figure index. The rate came into great prominence when at the turn of the century a really determined effort was made to develop the maternal and child welfare services as we now know them, and the early Medical Officers of Health of the towns were liable to be judged by what happened to the infant mortality rate. Better health services and the elimination of the grosser forms of poverty have changed the picture completely. In 1901 the pattern of infant mortality was as shown in Table Ten.

England and Wales 1901

TABLE TEN

Infant mortality. Deaths under one year per 1,000 live births

Cause	Rate
Measles	2
Whooping cough	5
Diarrhoeal diseases	34
Tuberculous diseases	6
Meningitis and convulsions	19
Pneumonia	10
Bronchitis	13
Wasting disease	46
Other causes	16
All causes	151

At this time infections, much more associated with environment and less with congenital factors, predominated, and deaths were

[1] Note that in this case it is the reciprocal of $m/{}^s m$ which is averaged, i.e. ${}^s m/m$.

generally spread over the first year of life. As environmental causes diminished interest was diverted to the residual and less tractable problem of endogenous causes of death. Such causes are associated with the uterine development of the foetus and the birth process itself—congenital malformation, prematurity and birth injury. The figures for England and Wales in 1960 are illustrative (Table Eleven).

These two groups of causes which account for about ninety-five per cent of all deaths in the first year differ widely in their age gradient. For the first group of constitutional and non-infective diseases nearly one-half of the infant deaths are in the first day and more than four-fifths are in the first week; for the second group of infections and accidents, only about one-seventh of the infant deaths are in the first week, and about three-quarters occur after the first four weeks.

Partly from consideration of these differential age gradients and partly on grounds of simplicity it became customary to separate deaths in the first four weeks of life as attributable to neo-natal mortality as distinct from later deaths which are classed as post-neo-natal. The neo-natal mortality rate is calculated in the same way as the infant mortality rate, viz. per 1,000 live births. The tremendous reduction in infant mortality since the turn of the century has been more attributable to post-natal mortality (infections diarrhoeal or respiratory and accidents) than to neo-natal mortality. Mortality from prematurity, congenital malformations or injury at birth has been more resistant to improvement.

More recently there has been a tendency to distinguish even more clearly the true natal deaths from those attributable to post-natal environmental influences by reference to deaths in the first week of life, and such deaths per 1,000 related live births provide an early neo-natal mortality rate. These deaths combined with stillbirths and rated to 1,000 total births can be regarded as measuring mortality at a period of time surrounding birth and may be described as peri-natal mortality.

The perinatal mortality rate has the advantage that, unlike its components, the still birth and early neo-natal rates, it is not likely to be disturbed by variations in the practice of recording or in the actual timing of foetal deaths. If a foetus is regarded as surviving beyond intra-uterine existence a death is transferred from the still-birth to the early neo-natal category though the actual reality of the situation—death around the point of delivery—is unaffected. This is quite an important point as the precise fixation of the time of foetal death is often difficult.

Infant Mortality England and Wales 1960

TABLE ELEVEN

Infant mortality per 1,000 related live births in age period

	under 1 day	1 day and under 1 week	1 week and under 4 weeks	4 weeks and under 3 months	3 months and under 6 months	6 months and under 1 year
Congenital malformations, birth injury, postnatal asphyxia and atelectasis, erythroblastosis, immaturity and ill-defined diseases peculiar to early infancy						
M.	8·19	6·04	1·46	0·88	0·50	0·29
F.	6·21	4·28	1·33	0·84	0·56	0·44
Pneumonia, bronchitis, gastroenteritis, other infective diseases, accidental mechanical suffocation, neglect, and other violent causes						
M.	0·18	0·64	0·77	1·58	1·51	1·17
F.	0·15	0·35	0·56	1·32	1·18	0·86

4

Occupational Mortality Investigations

The central problem of public health at the end of the nineteenth century, when the great plagues and pestilences had been banished by sanitary engineering, was really poverty. The link between poverty and disease began to impress itself on the social conscience and especially on the medical profession. It was natural therefore that mortality measurement should begin to be orientated toward the separation of the effects of social and economic factors. The General Register Office had carried out occupational mortality investigations by relating the deaths in years surrounding the decennial census to the populations in occupational groups revealed by the census (used as the mean population at risk) from 1851. These investigations gradually increased in definition as the reliability of occupational classification improved. Mention must also be made of the Manchester Unity Experience of 1893–7 which was the first analysis of the sickness and mortality experience of a friendly society to provide reliable data on occupational variation in the incidence of sickness claims. In this the following broad groups were analysed: agriculture, outdoor trades, railways, seafaring and fishing, quarry workers, iron and steel (heavy labour and exposure to heat), mining occupations (chiefly underground), remainder (rural), remainder (urban). But the main advance was provided by the occupational mortality investigation associated with years surrounding the 1911 census and carried out by Dr Stevenson of the General Register Office. In this investigation the occupations were combined into groups 'designed as far as possible to represent different social grades'. These groups were based on a subjective appraisal of the social esteem for the job rather than any objective assessment of the level of living (the census does not provide the data for such an assessment) and there are serious pitfalls in such an analysis (discrepancies between census and death registration records of occupation, absence of any durational factor in the analysis) but it was a real beginning in social differentiation. These so-called 'social classes' are now outmoded and they have been replaced by the more homogeneous and meaningful socio-economic groups but they have served their purpose well; they formed the basis of many important studies from which much valuable information was obtained about social and economic factors in mortality.

In calculating occupational rates of mortality we need to know not only the number of deaths for each cause by age and sex in each occupation (if possible by duration of engagement in the occupation) but also the relative population at risk, i.e. the average numbers engaged in the occupation similarly classified. On a national basis it is not yet possible to obtain information of duration of engagement in the occupation either at census or at death registration. Details of occupation are recorded at the census and, apart from the omission of the durational element, this enables populations at risk to be derived applicable to periods of time close to the census date. Occupation of the deceased is routinely furnished by the 'informant' at death registration and the Registrar General of England and Wales now regularly tabulates this information for years surrounding the census, and prepares a report on occupational mortality for this period as part of the Decennial Supplement. In 1931 the period 1930–2 was chosen but for the most recent published investigation (General Register Office 1958) the period 1949–53 was chosen to enable large numbers to be deployed; finer analysis could thus be made without diminishing the size of the groups to a point at which the rates become liable to relatively large chance errors.

Age Standardization

It is essential in any comparative study of occupational mortality to standardize for age. A crude death rate based on the total population claiming a particular occupation would be liable to mislead in two ways:

(a) The death rate in occupation A might be higher than that in occupation B although age for age mortality is higher in B simply because, for example, B happened to be a more youthful population either by virtue of reduced longevity or because it comprised a new occupation of fairly recent recruitment. As an example of the first cause the following figures are of interest.

Average annual death rates per 1,000 living at each age period 1910–12

	15–	20–	25–	35–	45–	55–	65–74	All ages 15–74
Farmers	0·5	1·5	3·1	4·6	8·6	20·0	51·3	11·6
Coal miners (hewers and getters)	3·2	3·8	4·4	6·7	12·7	30·1	82·3	9·3

The death rates at each age were higher for coal miners but by the same token they were a younger population than farmers and experienced a lower crude death rate.

(b) The total population claiming a particular occupation will include some too young to have incurred any real measure of occupational risk and many too old to have had any contact with the occupational hazard for many years prior to death (though to exclude them does lessen the weight given to post-poned efiects). In addition statements of occupation are particularly liable to be misleading for older persons.

It is therefore usual in the Registrar General's investigations to restrict consideration to the occupied and retired population of working ages, for example 20–65, and to allow for varying age structure within the range by standardization. Separate examination is made of males, single women and married women. The married women are classified by the occupation of their husbands.This is to provide a means of obtaining an indication of real occupational factors. If the wives show the same excess mortality as the husbands for a particular occupation it is implicit that a general environmental or socio-economic factor is involved rather than a true occupational hazard. The method of standardization normally employed is the 'standardized mortality ratio', i.e. age specific rates based on all males (or single women, etc.) are applied to the census population for the occupation to give a figure of 'standard' deaths, and the actual deaths are expressed as a ratio (the 'standardized mortality ratio') to the 'standard' deaths. This index is a ratio of 'actual' to 'expected' in a population not of standard structure but of a structure typical of the occupation and the term 'standardized' is not strictly appro-priate. This method was used in the 1931 and 1951 investigations. These operations are performed over the range 20–65.

Social Class Mortality

The occupational classification used by the Registrar General for census purposes comprises several hundred unit groups to which one or more individual occupations are assigned depending upon the description on the census schedule.

Each unit will be broadly homogeneous in respect of the job performed (for example manual or non-manual, machine or hand, skill involved) and the conditions in which it is performed (indoor or outdoor, clean or dirty, sedentary or ambulant, heat or cold, long or short hours, seasonal pressure, etc.). But for presenting differentials associated with general levels of living it is convenient to group units together (i) into *social classes* or (ii) *socio-economic groups*. These are described in detail in Chapter 11.

The socio-economic homogeneity of 'social classes' is limited by the fact that whole occupational units only are assigned to a group irrespective of the circumstances of individual workers coded to that unit, and by the fact that the assignment to social group is governed by the relative prestige of the occupation rather than by objective information of income, etc., which in any case is lacking in the census or registration data. Nevertheless the social classes do effect a broad division of the occupied population by economic and social circumstances. The socio-economic groups were introduced by the General Register Office at the 1951 Census as a new and alternative grouping to social classes and were extended at the 1961 Census. They represent an improvement in environmental homogeneity.

At the 1949–53 investigation the following gradients were discernible:

TABLE TWELVE

England and Wales standardized mortality ratios 1949–53

Ages 20–64	Social class				
	I	II	III	IV	V
Occupied males	98	86	101	94	118
Single women	82	73	89	89	92
Wives of males in specified social class	96	88	101	104	110

These social class gradients differed both in steepness and in direction for different causes of death. Causes for which mortality rose steeply with social class (i.e. with *less* favourable economic circumstances) included:

S.M.Rs. (males 20–64)	I	II	III	IV	V
Respiratory tuberculosis	58	63	102	95	143
Bronchitis	34	53	98	101	171
Pneumonia	53	64	92	105	150
Other myocardial degeneration	68	82	94	101	135
Ulcer of stomach	53	71	98	104	144
Malignant neoplasm, stomach	57	70	101	112	130

while the following are examples of causes apparently associated with comparative affluence:

	I	II	III	IV	V
Acute poliomyelitis	295	171	90	63	42
Leukaemia	123	98	104	93	89
Coronary disease, angina	147	110	105	79	89
Cirrhosis of liver	207	152	84	70	96
Diabetes	134	100	99	85	105
Vascular lesions of nervous system	124	104	101	88	101
Suicide	140	113	89	92	117

and some show very little gradient at all, as for example:

Nephritis and nephrosis   102   98   100   94   105

For the socio-economic groups of the 1951 census the S.M.Rs. were as shown in Table Thirteen.

TABLE THIRTEEN

Standard mortality ratios for socio-economic groups

Group (ages 20–64)	Standardized mortality ratios		
	Occupied	Wives of males in group	Single women
1. Farmers	70	93	72
2. Agricultural workers	75	95	64
3. Higher administrative, professional and managerial	98	96	82
4. Other administrative, professional and managerial	84	81	70
5. Shopkeepers (including proprietors of wholesale businesses)	100	99	97
6. Clerical workers	109	91	75
7. Shop assistants	84	79	82
8. Personal service	113	101	84
9. Foremen	84	91	86
10. Skilled workers	102	105	109
11. Semiskilled workers	97	108	99
12. Unskilled workers	118	111	103

Occupational Differences

The occupations with the twenty highest S.M.Rs. (all causes) among 425 occupational groups in the 1949–53 investigation were:

	S.M.R. of men 20–64	S.M.R. of wives (where given) 20–64
Royal Navy—other ranks (retired)	826	—
Army—other ranks (retired)	556	—
Royal Air Force—other ranks (retired)	485	—
Slate workers (not elsewhere specified); slate masons	467	300
Tunnel miners	225	(50)
Getters (mines) (not coal)	222	149
Armed forces—commissioned officers (retired)	189	—
Makers of glass and glassware—blowers (not machine hands or bench glass workers)	189	133

	S.M.R. of men 20–64	S.M.R. of wives (where given) 20–64
Drivers of horse drawn vehicles	189	170
Labourers and other unskilled workers in all other industrial and commercial undertakings	186	172
Haulage contractors and managers	175	168
Sand blasters (excluding shot blasters)	173	96
Machine minders—others	160	123
Managers (not elsewhere specified)	155	—
Workers in chemical and allied trades— furnacemen, kilnmen	154	164
In coal mines—hewers and getters (by hand)— below ground	153	146
Land agents, estate agents	150	165
Publicans, owners, etc., of hotels, inns	150	116
Curriers, leather dressers	149	135
Coal mines—coal face coal getters, loaders	148	143

Occupations with low mortality included, for example, farmers, farm managers (S.M.R. of males 20–64, 70) foremen, overlookers in metal manufacture and engineering (68), Civil Service higher officers (60), heads or managers of office departments (55), bankers, bank managers, inspectors (76), teachers (not music) (66), costing and accounting clerks (70).

For many occupations with low mortality the S.M.R. for the wives was also low, e.g. bankers, bank and insurance managers, etc. (husbands 78, wives 82), teachers (husbands 66, wives 77), clergymen of the Church of England (husbands 81, wives 80) indicating that it was not so much the occupation that was healthy as the level of living associated with the occupation. A similar argument (in the opposite direction) could be extended to some of the high mortality occupations in the 1949–53 analysis, e.g. the S.M.R. for the wives of drivers of horsedrawn vehicles (170), furnacemen, kilnmen in chemical trades (164), labourers (172), but in some instances there was a much greater excess mortality in husbands than in wives, e.g.

Husbands S.M.R.		Wives S.M.R.
173	Sandblasters	96
189	Glass blowers	133
160	Machine minders	123
150	Publicans, etc.	116

and this kind of contrast helps to establish prima facie evidence for closer enquiry.

DIFFICULTIES OF INTERPRETATION

The interpretation of occupational mortality data is much more difficult than the mere calculation of the indices, complicated though these may appear.

There are a number of sources of error and confusion:

(a) *Vagueness of Description and Coding Difficulties*

Occasional vagueness in the entry of occupation in census returns and death registers places a strain upon the capacity of the coding clerk to make a 'reproducible' assignment to an occupation unit, i.e. an assignment that would be made by any other coder faced with the same description; there is thus no guarantee that in such circumstances the same assignment would be made for the same person at census and at death. Nor is it certain that in cases of death soon after the census date the same description will be used since the informant may refer to the occupation carried out for the greater part of the lifetime of the deceased rather than to the occupation in which the deceased was most recently engaged. For example a police sergeant who retires comparatively early in life may take up a clerical occupation of a relatively minor character to supplement his pension and give him an active interest; at his death it is very likely that the widow or other relative will still consider him to be a retired police sergeant.

There is also a natural tendency for a householder completing a census schedule to elevate the status of his occupation, and for relatives to do the same at the registration of his death. This may take the form of using a description which implies a higher degree of skill or of supervisory capacity than is in fact applicable. If there were the same degree of elevation at both census and death registration there would be errors in the statistics of an absolute character but differentials would not be distorted. However, it has been found that the conditions under which the census is carried out—the prior propaganda, the instructions and examples on the census schedule, the fact that the occupation entry is only part of a more extended discipline (including reference to industry and workplace)—tend to make the census occupation entries more accurate than those made at registration. The absolute degree of error is not however great at working ages and the situation may generally be summarized by saying that status is slightly exaggerated at the census, is rather more exaggerated at death registration, but that the resultant bias in the direction of raising mortality in the higher grade occupations is not, for the ages for which indices are usually calculated, of serious consequence.

(b) Lack of Time Reference

The studies of occupational mortality are handicapped by the fact that the information both at census and at death is related in most cases to the immediately antecedent occupation. While the census information probably gives a fair approximation to the mean numbers at risk in the different occupations the deaths will be biased in the direction of lighter occupations to the extent to which failing health may lead workers to foresake heavier for lighter employment. The extent of this error is not known; it is probably corrected to some extent by tendency, noted above, to refer back to the occupation with which the deceased was associated for most of his life. Ideally, deaths and numbers at risk would be classified by duration of employment but the difficulties of obtaining accurate information even at the census, let alone at death registration, are too great to be overcome with present resources.

(c) Separation of Specific Occupation Factors

Reference has already been made to the difficulty of deciding whether excess mortality is due to occupational risk or general social environment and of the use, for example, of the mortality of wives as a control. The mortality index even thus controlled can do no more than establish a prima facie case for closer study within the particular occupation.

THE LIFE TABLE

We noted in the introductory chapters that an important way of summarizing a mortality experience is by means of the life table, i.e. a table which shows, on the basis of current mortality rates, the number out of 1,000 births (or some other convenient starting number, termed the 'radix' of the table) who survive to certain specified ages and the numbers dying between these successive points of age. A full life table gives this information for each integral age from nought to an upper limit beyond which it is convenient to regard the number of survivors as negligible. (As it is impractical to have a fraction of a survivor it is necessary to choose a radix large enough to allow for whole numbers to be surviving at these advanced ages.) Shorter tables (abridged life tables) are commonly produced which give the survivors and deaths for five year intervals. Table Three is an example of an abridged table based on the mortality of England and Wales, 1952.

NOTATION

The symbol l_x is conventionally used to denote the number surviving to the exact age x and d_x is used to indicate the number dying between exact age x and the next age shown in the table. $l_{x+1} = l_x - d_x$. The average number alive between age x and $x + 1$ is denoted by L_x. This is the average of l_x for all values of x between exact age x and exact age $x + 1$, i.e. $\int_0^1 l_{x+t} \cdot dt$. Alternatively we can regard this expression as measuring the total years of life lived between x and $x + 1$ by those who attain age x. This is a better explanation of why L_x is used as the denominator of the central death rate m_x referred to below.

Other symbols are:

$m_x =$ the death rate at age x last birthday in the ordinary vital statistics sense of the ratio of annual deaths at age x last birthday to the average population at age x last birthday during the period of measurement. An average population at risk is involved for which a mid-period population is often used as an approximation. This is sometimes referred to as a *central* death rate.

$q_x =$ the probability of dying within one year of attaining exact age x, i.e. d_x/l_x.

$p_x =$ the probability of surviving at least one year after attaining exact age x, i.e. l_{x+1}/l_x. (The word 'probability' here is used merely in the sense of the proportionate mortality or survival and p_x and q_x are expressed as proportions *per unit* so that $p_x + q_x = 1$. If $p_x = 0.5$ this means that according to the life table one half of those who attain age x also survive to age $x + 1$.)

$T_x =$ the total population aged x and over in a stationary population generated by constant births and subject to the life table mortality. From what has been said already about L_x it will be seen that T_x is the cumulative sum of L_x for all values of x up to the end of the table.

$\mathring{e}_x =$ the complete expectation of life, i.e. the average period in years (including fractions of a year) lived beyond age x by those who attain exact age x, $\mathring{e}_x = T_x/l_x$.

RATES OF MORTALITY AND PROBABILITIES OF DEATH

The two functions m_x and q_x represent different concepts. The first represents the average risk to which the population is subjected during its passage through the year of age x to $x + 1$; the second represents the total effect of the mortality pressure in terms of those who fail to survive the whole year without reference to its variation over the course of that year. The two measures are related by the fact that

$$m_x = \frac{d_x}{\int_0^1 l_{x+t} \cdot dt} \quad \text{and} \quad q_x = \frac{d_x}{l_x}.$$

If the deaths are uniformly distributed over the year of age (as they are, approximately, except at birth and at extreme old age) then $\int_0^1 l_{x+t} \cdot dt$ (or L_x) is approximately the population of the middle of the year of age, viz. $l_{x+\frac{1}{2}} = l_x - \frac{1}{2}d_x$.

We may then write

$$m_x = \frac{d_x}{l_x - \frac{1}{2}d_x}$$

$$= (d_x/l_x) - [1 - \frac{1}{2} \cdot (d_x/l_x)]$$

$$= q_x \div 1 - \frac{1}{2} \cdot q_x$$

and

$$q_x = \frac{2m_x}{2 + m_x}, \quad p_x = \frac{2 - m_x}{2 + m_x}$$

Thus when m_x has been derived, the values of q_x and p_x required to produce the life table may be derived from these simple relationships.

When the column of p_x has been derived it is a simple matter to start with a convenient radix $l_0 = 100,000$ and to find $l_1 = l_0 \times p_0$, $l_2 = l_1 \times p_1$, etc.

It should be noted that since $d_x = l_{x+1} - l_x$ by definition, then $l_x = d_x + d_{x+1} + d_{x+2}. \ldots$

Actuarial Methods

Life tables themselves have no greater mystery about them than any other statistical tables showing the frequency of occurrence of specified events or of numbers of persons in specified categories. Any difficulty arises mainly in the calculation of the appropriate population at risk corresponding to the observed deaths from which it is proposed to derive the basic death rates—or probabilities of death if these are to be derived directly. The fundamental techniques for this purpose especially where the data are not in census form require more extended treatment than can be accommodated here and reference should be made to appropriate textbooks.

There are however one or two matters of methodology to be stressed. In the first year of life, mortality is varying rapidly and in calculating a life table it is necessary to break up the year of age into intervals during which more uniform mortality may be assumed and to calculate q directly for these intervals by having regard to the related births, i.e. those among which the deaths may be assumed to have occurred.

As an example of this method reference may be made to the Decennial Supplement of the Registrar General for England and

Wales 1931, Part I, Life Tables, p. 28 where it will be seen that for English Life Table No. 10 (deaths of 1930–32 and census population 1931)

$$q_0 = q_0^{(0-3 \text{ months})} + q_0^{(3-6 \text{ months})} + q_0^{(6-9 \text{ months})} + q_0^{(9-12 \text{ months})}$$

where $q_0^{(0-3 \text{ months})}$ = probability of dying in the first quarter of the first year

$$= \frac{\text{deaths in 1930, 1931 and 1932 (age 0–3 months)}}{\frac{1}{2}b_{1929}^4 + b_{1930} + b_{1931} + b_{1932} - \frac{1}{2}b_{1932}^4}$$

where b_{1929}^4 = births in fourth quarter of 1929 which would on the average be exposed to risk of death at age 0–3 months for one half of the following quarter.

(Note also that reference back to births was also necessary for those ages which corresponded to generations born at times of sharp fluctuation in the birth rate, for here again in the absence of stability it is not possible to assume that the mid population is also the average population.)

At advanced ages the data are always scanty and age statements are unreliable. It is usual therefore to assume an arbitrary trend to run off the table either by fitting a mathematical curve to the later part of the q_x column or drawing a freehand curve and extrapolating. It is common to adopt a curve named after Gompertz who used it to express a law of mortality, viz. $m_x = Bc^x$ where B and c are constants. Any degree of approximation adopted is not important since the values of the rates at these advanced ages have little effect on expectations of life over the main body of the table.

Methods of Calculating Abridged Life Tables

For many purposes it is unnecessary to undertake the labour of producing a full life table with all the many refinements that may be necessary to avoid chance irregularities in the progression of probabilities of death from one age to another. The main summary character of the table may be achieved by producing the abridged form especially where it is only desired to make broad comparisons between successive years in the same country or between different countries at the same period of time.

Various methods of calculating abridged life tables have been suggested. Of those the following have been chosen for illustrative purposes.

E. C. Snow's Method

Snow's approach (1914) was to find empirical relations, based on pre-existing tables, between $m_{x,t}$ and $_tp_x$, and between

$$\frac{1}{l_x}\sum_0^4 l_{x+t} \quad \text{and} \quad _tp_x$$

Thus we have, for 5 year groups, the scheme shown on p. 100. $m_{x,t}$ is calculated in the normal way from grouped data. $_tp_x$ is then obtained from tabulated values and l_x follows directly. Values of $\sum_0^t \frac{l_{x+t}}{l_x}$ are taken from the standard tables and $\sum_0^t l_{x+t}$ follows by multiplication by l_x. $\mathring{e}_x$ is obtained from relation

$$\mathring{e}_x = \left[\frac{l_x + l_{x+1} + \cdots}{l_x}\right] - \frac{1}{2}$$

This method, while very rapid, may not apply to different countries or periods of time and experiments would be needed before it could be safely used.

Greville's Abridged Life Tables (1943)

Transition from $m_{x,t}$ to $q_{x,t}$ is effected by

$$q_{x,t} = \frac{m_{x,t}}{\dfrac{1}{t} + m_{x,t}\left[\dfrac{1}{2} + \dfrac{t}{12}(m_{x,t} - 0\cdot 09)\right]}$$

(The constant $0\cdot 09$ is alternative to $\log_e c$ where c is derived by fitting Gompertz's Law $m_{x,t} = Bc^x$ to $m_{x,t}$.) Rates of mortality for initial ages are found by births and deaths to obtain a starting value of l_x and then the abridged method is applied. L_x is obtained from the relationship

$$\sum_0^t L_{x+t} = \frac{\sum_0^t d_{x+t}}{m_{x+t}}$$

assuming that $m_{x,t}$ applies to the life table population as to the actual population whence T_x is found by summing back from the highest age, and thence $\mathring{e}_x$.

U.S. Abridged Life Tables (1945)

This method, also attributable to Greville, involves construction of an abridged table by reference to a standard full table—in this case the U.S. 1939–41 Table. It is assumed that the $m_{x,t}:q_{x,t}$

Ages over ten

Range of death rate $m_{x,5}$	Equation for $_5p_x$	Range of $_5p_x$	Equation for $\dfrac{1}{l_x}\left(\sum_0^4 l_{x+t}\right)$
0–0·00300	$_5p_x = 0\cdot99995 - 4\cdot8883m$		
0·00300–0·00370	$_5p_x = 0\cdot98152 + 5095\cdot5(0\cdot00383 - m_{x,5})^2$		
0·00370–0·00550	$_5p_x = 0\cdot95419 + 247\cdot824(0\cdot01423 - m_{x,5})^2$	$1\cdot0 - 0\cdot9750$	$\dfrac{1}{l_x}\left(\sum_0^4 l_{x+t}\right) = 3\cdot0914 + 1\cdot9084\,_5p_x$

Ages under ten

5–10	$_5p_5 = 0\cdot99838 - 4\cdot68161m_{5,5}$	$\dfrac{1}{l_5}\sum_5^9 l_t = 2\cdot2504 + 2\cdot7556\,_5p_5$
2–5	$_3p_2 = 0\cdot99883 - 2\cdot78684m_{2,3}$	$\dfrac{1}{l_2}\sum_2^4 l_t = 1\cdot4959 + 1\cdot5105\,_3p_2$
1–2	$p_1 = 0\cdot07434 + 0\cdot92488\dfrac{(2 - m_1)}{2 + m_1}$	
0–1	$p_0 = 1 -$ (infant deaths per birth)	

relationship in the standard table may be applied to the particular calendar year for which an abridged table its required apart from

(i) the terminal age group 75+, where it is assumed that $\mathring{e}_{75} = r/m_{75}$, r being the ratio of the terminal group death rate in the actual data of standard table to that of the standard table population.

(ii) q_0 which is calculated directly from death and birth data.

ΣL_x is derived by using the standard table ratios

$$\frac{t \cdot l_x - \sum\limits_0^t L_{x+t}}{\sum\limits_0^t d_{x+t}}$$

on values of l_x and d_x of the abridged table, on the assumption that these ratios remain unchanged when the abridged table values are substituted for those of the standard table.

Current General Register Office Abridged Life Table

This is published annually in the December Quarterly Return and is constructed from estimated home population in any period and total deaths registered in that period.

Values of l_x and $\mathring{e}_x$ are given for individual ages up to five and then at five-yearly intervals up to age eighty-five.

$m_{x,5}$ is converted to $_5p_x$ by the relationship

$$_5p_x = \frac{2 - 5m_{x,t}}{2 + 5m_{x,t}}$$

except at ages one to four where the individual age relationship $p = \dfrac{2 - m}{2 + m}$ is used and at age nought where the first year of life is subdivided into 0–, 1–, 3–, 6–, 9–12 months and infant mortality is calculated on the basis of related births to give q_0 by summation.

ΣL_x is obtained by assuming l_x to be linear over each interval of time used whence T_x and $\mathring{e}_x$.

Expectation of Life

The word 'expectation' can only be applied appropriately to measurement of lifetime in the sense that the 'expectation of life' is the average number of years lived by people 'in the long run'. In practice we do not know what might happen 'in the long run' because mortality is constantly changing and we cannot observe the 'long run' under stable conditions. Nothing is more certain than that the mortality of the past will not be reproduced in the future. Yet we find it convenient to consider the average lifetime of those

TABLE FOURTEEN

Expectation of life according to
abridged life table, 1952 (home population),
England and Wales

Age	Males	Females
0	67·06	72·35
1	68·20	73·14
2	67·35	72·27
3	66·44	71·34
4	65·51	70·40
5	64·56	69·44
10	59·74	64·58
15	54·88	59·69
20	50·12	54·83
25	45·44	50·03
30	40·72	45·27
35	36·02	40·52
40	31·39	35·84
45	26·86	31·26
50	22·57	26·82
55	18·64	22·57
60	15·11	18·52
65	11·97	14·76
70	9·27	11·38
75	6·96	8·45
80	5·15	6·09
85	3·62	4·35

who have recently died as a guide to future expectation and it is useful and fair to do so within limitations.

We must also take note that expectation of life has no meaning at all, not even an approximate one, except in relation to some starting age, because at later ages the weaker members of the population have died and the surviving population represent a select body with better prospects of longevity. This may not be commonly appreciated. It might be thought perhaps that since the expectation of life at birth (i.e. calculated from birth) was sixty-seven years for men, then all men reaching age sixty-five have two further years to live on the average. In fact, however, the expectation at birth is calculated by averaging the lifetimes of all males born, some of whom die *before* sixty-five; whereas the expectation of life at sixty-five is calculated only in relation to those who die *after* age sixty-five and this select band of men live, on average, for another twelve years. A simple example will make this clear. Suppose our population under observation consists of four[1] men who die at ages 55, 59, 66 and 88. These four men at the time of their birth were destined to live on the average for $\frac{1}{4}(55 + 59 + 66 + 88) = 67$ years. So we say the expectation at birth is sixty-seven. On the other hand, starting from age sixty-five, we only consider those who are still alive (those who are dead have no expectation), viz.: those who die at sixty-six and eighty-eight, and these live one and twenty-three years, i.e. an average of twelve years, beyond age sixty-five. The expectation of life at age sixty-five, $\dot{e}_{65}$, is thus 12. In quoting expectations of life it is essential to specify the age beyond which the expectation is calculated.

Longitudinal Studies—Survival Factors

At the beginning of this century a new problem had emerged; tuberculosis was killing large numbers of adults and most of them died young. In the early days little could be done to arrest the relentless progress of the disease and efforts were concentrated upon the detection of cases and on the isolation of the infectious patients. Later as the possibility of curative treatment began to be probed it was necessary to establish careful systems of surveillance to measure the risks of relapse or death in different treatment groups. Orthodox actuarial methods were employed, the deaths in each year of duration from treatment being related to the number surviving in that year of duration. The main problem was to reduce to a minimum the number of patients 'lost sight of' and, in respect of these, to make appropriate deductions from the exposed-to-risk which formed the denominator of the death rate in any year of duration. The index prepared for each group was the proportion surviving at the end of x years.

Later the method was developed as a means of assessing the effects of treatment of cancer, another disease following a comparatively

---

[1] We would not actually be so foolish as to calculate an expectation based on a handful of lives—the calculations are normally based on hundreds of thousands of completed lives (deaths).

slow course which presented a problem of growing proportions as the average length of life increased.

Generation Mortality Tables

The continuing improvement in almost all causes of death at most ages together with the wealth of mortality experience by then accumulated, led actuaries, especially in the period between the two World Wars, to turn seriously to the problem of forecasting the future changes in mortality. In this process emphasis was given to the fact that a comparison of successive life tables might be misleading. The normal life table based on the deaths of a limited period is not likely to be reproduced in the future; it mixes the experience of a number of different generations—the lives who contribute to the death rates at advanced ages were born many decades before those who contribute to the rates at young ages, and they have lived through conditions which are unlikely to be replicated for later generations. This defect can be remedied when mortality records have been maintained over a long period and a life table can be based on the experience of a single generation following it through from birth to extinction. The method is exactly the same as for normal life table calculations except that the death rates ought to be taken from a tabulation of death rates according to calendar year of *birth* and year of age passed through. Such an explicit tabulation is not normally available but as an approximation we might say that for those born (say) in 1870–74 (and using earlier notation) $m_{30,5}$, for example, would be based on death rates at ages 30–34 observed in the period 1900–09 when the generation passed through this age group or, at least, observed in years centred at the midpoint of this period.

Approximating in this way it is common to base the generation mortality table on the diagonals of a tabulation of the following kind. The columns of such a table are the group death rates as published, for example, in the annual statistical review of the Registrar General of England and Wales.

Period of observation of mortality

Age	1870–74	1875–79	1880–84	1885–89	etc.
0–4	$m_{0,5}$				
5–9		$m_{5,5}$			
10–14			$m_{10,5}$		
15–19				$m_{15,5}$	
etc.					

Years of Life Lost

The movement of the impact of preventable mortality to middle life and the new problem of the lack of improvement in the mortality of older men has led to the development of another method of presenting mortality which serves to emphasize the loss of active life involved. The aim is to consider the years of life lost by each death rather than to simply count the number of persons whose lives were terminated; the underlying concept being that a man dying at the age of say thirty might but for the 'accident' of death have lived to the remainder of his normal span and that it might be a greater achievement to prevent his death than to save the life of a man aged ninety who cannot have much longer to live.

There is the problem of the choice of the 'normal span of life' to be used in measuring years lost on death. There is no precise or absolute measure since a current life table is necessarily based upon the mortality of the lives now dying and is never exactly reproduced; and any 'projected' life table would be entirely arbitrary and speculative. We may take refuge in the fact that the assessment of mortality improvement requires relative indices rather than absolute measures and simply adopt a reasonable estimate of span based upon current experience. It would be possible for example to take as the limit of 'normal' life that age in the life table at which the number of lives surviving is less than ten per cent of the original entrants, viz. the maximum span within which ninety per cent of persons die and is survived only by an abnormally longeval ten per cent. For males this is eighty-five and for females eighty-eight years of age in round numbers and at current levels of mortality. The Registrar General, in calculating the index for England and Wales which is published in the Quarterly Return for the second quarter of each year, uses age eighty-five for both sexes as a simplification. He distributes the years of life between the working age period, fifteen to sixty-four, and the remainder. For a man dying at age twenty it would therefore be assumed that a total potential loss of years of life (for index purposes only) of sixty-five years was incurred, and forty-five of those years would be in the working age range. On this basis the mortality of 1965 represented for males a total loss of 235 years, and a loss of seventy-one working years, per thousand population. For females the total loss was 146 years, and the working life lost was forty-three years, per 1,000 population.

REFERENCES

History

Greenwood, M. *Medical Statistics from Graunt to Farr*, Cambridge University Press (1948).

Indices
Haenszel, W. *American Journal of Public Health*, 40, 17 (1950).
Karn, M. N. *Annals of Eugenics*, 4, 279 (1931).
Kohn, R. *Canadian Journal of Public Health*, 42, 375 (1951).
Liddell, F. D. K. *British Journal of Industrial Medicine*, 17, 228 (1960).
Logan, W. P. D. and Benjamin, B. *Monthly Bulletin of the Ministry of Health and Public Health Laboratory Service*, 244 (December 1953).
Snow, D. J. R. *Report of the Commissioner for Public Health, West Australia 1951* (1953).
Yerushalmy, J. *American Journal of Public Health*, 41, 907 (1950).

Environmental factors
Antonosky, A. *Milbank Memorial Foundation Quarterly*, 45, 31 (1967).
Benjamin, B. *British Journal of Tuberculosis*, 47, 4 (1953).
Benjamin, B. *Social and Economic Factors in Mortality*, Volume V, *Confluence*. Mouton, Paris (1965).
Butler, N. R. and Bonham, D. G. *Perinatal Mortality*. E. & S. Livingstone, London (1963).
Regional and Social Factors in Infant Mortality, Studies in Population and Medical Subjects No. 19. General Register Office (1967).
Scott, J. A. *British Journal of Social and Preventive Medicine*, 7, 194 (1953).

Recent trends
Proceedings of the World Population Conference 1965, Volume II. United Nations (1967).

Life tables
Greville, T. N. E. *Record of American Institute of Actuaries*, 32, 29 (1943).
Snow, E. C. *Supplement to 75th Annual Report of the Registrar General* (1914).

8

Migration

OF the three elements in population change, births, deaths and migration, migration is much more variable from country to country in its importance and much more variable in the accuracy with which it is measured than the other two elements.

Some countries, like Ireland and Scotland, traditionally export manpower and would have serious unemployment problems if they did not do so. Other countries import manpower; Australia, at present, can barely get all the immigrants needed to develop natural resources and industries. Some new countries like Israel have been built up almost entirely on the basis of an immigrant resettled population. Mauritius has too many people; Guyana has too few. In general the redistribution of population by migration makes little difference to the problems of population pressure but is often, in particular cases, essential to economic development; some rapidly developing countries need immigrant manpower to exploit the full potential of capital and resources while, in contrast, some of the under-developed but overcrowded countries need to relieve the population pressure which impedes economic growth. The importance of migration to England and Wales has varied considerably. During the latter part of the nineteenth century and the early part of this century, England and Wales was a net exporter of labour all over the world and especially to Australasia, Africa, Canada and India. After the World economic depression around 1930 this flow was reversed. For many years after World War II net migration was relatively insignificant; from 1951–5 there was an average loss of 16,000 a year and from 1955–9 an average gain of 22,000 a year. In 1960 there began a mounting flow of immigration mainly from the Caribbean, India and Pakistan. In the year ended June 30, 1962 there was a net immigration from overseas of 195,000. Controls were imposed by the Commonwealth Immigrants Act of 1962 and the flow has subsided.

Variation in the accuracy of measurement arises partly because some countries which attract immigrants have imposed selective controls in order to get the kind of people they want while other countries have had no problem either of direction or volume of movement and have not found it necessary to institute any checks; and partly because in some countries there are systems of continuous population registration (i.e. registration of all changes in location of individuals) while others do not record the location of individuals except on the occasion of population censuses. Where there is a system of continuous population registration as for example in some Eastern European countries and in the Netherlands and Scandinavia, every movement, both within the country and across the boundaries of the country, will be recorded. There will not only be an exact count of movements within a specified time interval but also a full record of the characteristics (sex, age, occupation, destination and origin, etc.) of each mover. Where there is only a system of controls the information may be more restricted; only those movements subject to control will be recorded and the information recorded for each mover will be limited to that essential to the administrative process of control. Thus it is possible that only immigrants will be controlled and emigrants will not be covered. Where census information is used this may show the characteristics and the origins of those who admit to having moved within the last year or last five years but it will clearly not include those who have left the country and who are not there to be covered by the census information. Of course where censuses are carried out simultaneously in a number of different countries there is the possibility of reciprocal arrangements so that information on movements from country A to country B can be posted back to country A from the census data of country B. (This is certainly possible as between England and Wales, Scotland and Northern Ireland.) The degree of census simultaneity is small so that the recovery of emigration data by this means is clearly limited.

In England and Wales there has been no system of continuous population registration since National Registration was abandoned in 1952 and no system of immigration control for Commonwealth immigrants until 1962. Aliens have been compelled to register but they have formed only a proportion of the total volume of immigration. Until recently a rough picture was built up from the following scraps of information:

(a) The overall balance of passenger movement through sea and air ports. There were many sources of error especially at seasonal peaks when port passenger facilities were overloaded.

(b) Statistics from the manifests of ships of long sea routes.

Until the abolition in 1964 of the statutory requirement (Sec. 76 of the Merchant Shipping Act, 1906), ships' captains on these routes were required to indicate, in addition to other details of passengers, the country of last permanent residence and the country of future permanent residence. Permanent residence was defined as one used or intended to be used for at least 12 months.

(c) Registration of aliens.

(d) New issues and surrenders of National Health Service medical cards.

All this information was partial; source (b) became increasingly inadequate as long distance air travel became more popular. Nevertheless experienced handling of these sources did yield surprisingly accurate estimates as judged by comparison with the census estimates of population change after excluding the element due to natural increase.

The International Passenger Survey

The present main source of information is the International Passenger Survey. The Social Survey is commissioned by the Board of Trade to interview a stratified random sample of passengers entering and leaving the United Kingdom on all the principal air and sea routes (other than to the Irish Republic) to obtain information about migration, tourism and the contribution of travel expenditure to the balance of payments.

The sampling fractions are:

London Airport and Prestwick. 7 per cent of outgoing and 4 per cent of incoming passengers on long air routes. 2 per cent in winter and 1 per cent in summer, of short air route passengers.

Smaller airports. Between 0·5 and 4 per cent, according to time and airport concerned. Sample weights are adjusted for known traffic densities and appropriate allowance made for traffic not covered.

Short sea routes. About 1 per cent of winter and 0·5 per cent of summer traffic. In a two stage sample, cross-channel boats are sampled in proportion to the weight of traffic they are expected to handle and a predetermined number of passengers is interviewed on each selected boat.

Long sea routes. Every liner or other ship with more than 200 passengers arriving, or more than 100 departing, is covered and so is 1 out of every 2 other ships carrying more than 12 passengers on these routes. 7 per cent of the outgoing and 4 per cent of incoming passengers are sampled.

In deriving figures of intending immigrants and emigrants the criterion of intending to stay more than a year is adopted as the conventional definition distinguishing a migrant from other passengers.

Normally each year there are about 100,000 successful voluntary interviews with incoming passengers of whom perhaps 5,000 are identified as intending immigrants and about 125,000 voluntary interviews of outgoing passengers of whom about 12,500 may be intending emigrants. But the sample of intending immigrants may be grossed up some 40 times and of intending emigrants 20 times so that margins of error are likely to be substantial particularly when attempts are made to subdivide the data, for example to look at the occupational distribution of migrants.

The data on migration from the International Passenger Survey are published in the Quarterly Return of the Registrar General for England and Wales for the third quarter of each year. The tables cover migration into and out of the United Kingdom (separately)

(a) according to country of last or intended future residence,
(b) by occupation group and, within occupation group, broad age groups,
(c) by sex, age and citizenship (i.e. British, Commonwealth, or Alien),
(d) by sex, citizenship, and route travelled (i.e. long or short, sea or air),
(e) by sex, age, and marital condition,
(f) by sex, occupation and citizenship.

Regional Distribution of Migration—International and Internal

There is considerable interest not only in the balances of migration for different countries, for different sex, age and marital condition groups and for different occupation groups but also in the variation, within England and Wales, of migration balances. Undue immigration into a particular area may create a severe local housing problem. A heavy outflow of labour can produce employment imbalances and economic difficulties. This means that we are concerned not only with international migration but also internal migration, between one region and another. It is possible from the International Travel Survey data to distribute the international movements, and their balance, between regions. The internal migration is more difficult to deal with and certainly there is no information from which to derive the gross movement—the separate inter-region inward and outward movements. The overall balance may be estimated by subtracting the natural increase (excess of births over deaths) from the total population change for the area as provided by the local population estimate calculation (see p. 112). If the international migration balance is subtracted from the overall migration, the residual is the balance of movement due to internal migration. It should be borne in mind that we are dealing here with differences between quantities that are themselves subject to substantial margins of error; the net balances themselves will be subject therefore to even greater margins of error.

Census Information on Internal Migration

Useful information about the main streams of internal migration may be obtained from the census if questions are asked about changes of usual residence within a specified period (see p. 27). Tabulations derived from a question of this type will indicate not only the number of persons (or households) moving from one specified area to another within a defined interval of time but also the characteristics of the movers (and the households containing them). If these flows appear to be stable it may be possible to project them (i.e. specific to particular population groups) into the future (see p. 117). If there is no question on actual movement there may nevertheless be a question on the duration since last movement, i.e. since movement to the present usual residence. The tabulation of data derived from such a question will at least indicate the relative mobility of different groups in the population. Census tabulations by birthplace and usual residence also throw some light on mobility.

REFERENCES

Carrier, N. H. and Jeffery, J. R. *External Migration—A Study of the Available Statistics 1815–1950*, Studies in Population and Medical Subjects No. 6. General Register Office (1953).

Isaac, J. *British Post-war Migration*. Cambridge University Press (1954).

Newton, M. P. and Jeffery, J. R. *Internal Migration*, Studies in Population and Medical Subjects No. 5. General Register Office (1951).

Proceedings of the World Population Conference 1965, Volume IV. United Nations (1967).

9

Population estimation and projection

Intercensal Estimates of Total Population

The population is only counted at census years and if it is desired to estimate the population appropriate to an intercensal year some assumption must be made as to the rate of growth of the population during the intercensal period.

(a) If migration data are available then they may be combined with the natural increase to compute the population in any given year. If the information is available this is the safest method particularly if the intercensal period comprises, for example, a sudden fluctuation due to war or economic causes, and does not follow the stable trend exhibited in the last preceding intercensal period.

(b) Failing information as to migration it may be assumed that intercensal growth is either in:

(i) arithmetical progression, i.e. a constant *absolute* annual increase in population. If the population in 1921 is 154,000 and in 1931 is 160,000 it is assumed that the population is increasing by $\dfrac{160,000 - 154,000}{10} = 600$ per year, and hence that the population in 1925 may be estimated as $154,000 + 4(600) = 156,000$; or

(ii) geometrical progression, i.e. a constant percentage of its *attained* size each year. This takes account of the fact that accession of population means more parents producing children and a proportionate increase in the size of the succeeding absolute increment. (The difference between (a) and (b) is the difference between simple and compound

112

interest.) If r = annual rate of increase then for the same example,

$$160,000 = 154,000r^{10}$$

or $\quad \log r_{10} = \tfrac{1}{10}(\log_{10} 160,000 - \log_{10} 154,000)$

$$= 0 \cdot 00166 \quad \text{or} \quad r = 1 \cdot 004$$

Hence population in 1925 is

$$\log_{10}^{-1}[5 \cdot 18752 + 4(0 \cdot 00166)] \quad \text{or} \quad 156,370$$

Such estimates as these may be erroneous when applied to the entire country, and are still more likely to be in error for a local area such as a town which may, in an industrial boom, gain a rapid increase of working people with many children in a short time, followed immediately by a period of stability as the boom passes with migration balancing natural increase.

(c) Even if data on migration are lacking, other sources of information may be drawn upon to indicate the direction and pace of growth, such as the list of Parliamentary electors (rated up by their proportion to the entire population at the last census) or local registers of the number of rateable dwellings (multiplied by the average number of inhabitants in each house).

Estimates by Sex and Age

The need to produce estimates of population in sex and age groups implies a degree of sophistication in statistical organization and we assume that for example, to produce an estimate as at the middle of the year following census year, the following data are available:

(a) Estimate (itself census derived) at mid-point of census year (the method of moving from census date to mid-year is essentially the same as that here described for moving from mid-year to mid-year—see below for details) at individual ages last birthday for each sex, $-p_x$.

(b) Emigrants and immigrants from mid-year (census year) to mid-year (year of estimate) for each sex at individual ages as at mid-year (year of estimate); balance (+ for net inward movement, − for outward) denoted by m_x.

(c) Births, for each sex; occurrences from mid-year (census year) to mid-year (year of estimate), b_0.

(d) Deaths, for each sex, and at individual ages last birthday at mid-year (*year of estimate*), d_x, i.e. the age they would but for death have attained at the *end* of the year of movement.

Then

$$p_x \text{ (mid-year of estimate)} = p_{x-1} \text{ (mid census year)} + m_x - d_x$$

Where in the case of m and d the x relates to mid-year of estimate and the *end* of year of movement, and the ages are age last birthday, and for the first year of age

$$p_0 = b_0 + m_0 - d_0$$

The Use of "Total" Population

The process is carried out for each sex separately and is applied to the *total* population including Forces overseas (but excluding foreign forces stationed in the country). The reason for this is that were the process to be applied to the civilian population or to the actual population resident in the country (i.e. including national and foreign forces in the country but excluding national forces temporarily stationed overseas) the gap in the age structure caused by the temporary absence of this young segment of the population would be 'aged' whereas of course by virtue of its continuous replenishment its age structure remains virtually the same from year to year. Estimates of the *total* population are therefore derived as basic data and the civilian and 'home' (or actual) populations are derived by making the appropriate subtractions and additions. The total population may be looked upon as, approximately, the population owing allegiance to the government of the country (it omits visitors abroad and wrongly includes visitors to the country). The 'home' population is the population which would be counted in the national census.

Movement from Year to Year

The estimate for the middle of the following year is obtained by moving forward one year in exactly the same way. The process is continued until the next census provides a fresh benchmark from which to work.

The following figures are selected lines for the calculation of the mid-year estimates for males in England and Wales for mid 1966 (thousands).

The Base Population

It will be borne in mind that in moving from census day to mid-year in the initial adjustment of the new benchmark, the census population must (by interpolation) be redistributed by age attainable on 30 June and the movements, also distributed by age attained (or which they would have attained) at 30 June, will relate to the

TABLE FIFTEEN

Calculation of mid-year estimate of male population, England and Wales (thousands)

Age mid-1965	Mid-1965 estimate of total population	1965–66					Mid-1966 estimate			
		Age mid-1966	Net migration	Deaths	Net movement	Total	British non-civilians home and overseas	Civilian	Non-civilians in England and Wales	Home (including all non-civilians in civilians in England and Wales)
Births 1965–66	438·73	0	+0·02	−8·20	−8·18	430·55	—	430·55	—	430·55
0	437·52	1	−0·49	−1·43	−1·92	435·60	—	435·60	—	435·60
1	433·26	2	−0·47	−0·45	−0·92	432·34	—	432·34	—	432·34
19	355·41	20	+1·09	−0·39	+0·70	356·11	35·30	320·81	19·30	340·11

period from census date to 30 June. Thus if census day is 1 April we have

$$p_x \text{ (mid-census year)} = p_{x-\frac{1}{2}} \text{ (census date)} + m_x - d_x$$

where in the case of m and d, x relates to 30 June.

The census population is usually graduated or smoothed by fitting a curve to the distribution or using a graduation formula based on the principle of moving averages, and it is therefore possible to extend this same process to carry out the redistribution referred to above.

Age Distribution of Migrants

The migration figures are themselves likely to be estimates (see p. 107) and refinement in the distribution by age in the processes described above would rarely be justified. A fairly arbitrary allocation would in most cases be adequate especially where, as in England and Wales, the net migration is at any age small in relation to deaths. It will however be borne in mind that in England and Wales the migration element is a weak link in the calculation. Where therefore an estimate at census date (derived from the immediately previous intercensal year) is used as a check on the census total, the 'error' may merely reflect accumulated error in the estimate due to errors in estimating net migration (see p. 50).

Deaths

Where the deaths are recorded on punched cards or computer tape and the record includes either (a) the date of birth, or (b) the age at death together with the date of death, the requisite tabulation can be derived without difficulty. In the case (a) we need only to aggregate deaths of those born between 1 July of year (y), and 30 June of year ($y + 1$) to obtain for the year of movement (z) to ($z + 1$), where the bracketed symbols relate to specific calendar years, the number represented by d_{z-y}. In the case of (b) we would assume an even flow of deaths over the year of age x to $x + 1$ and therefore that those aged x last birthday were all born $x + \frac{1}{2}$ years prior to the date of death. We might further assume for this purpose that deaths are evenly spread over the calendar year for the year of movement (z) to ($z + 1$) thus average date of occurrence is 31 December (z) when they were aged x last birthday or approximately $x + \frac{1}{2}$ exact. This means that to obtain d_x we take $\frac{1}{2}$[deaths at age (x) last birthday in year of movement plus deaths at age ($x - 1$) last birthday in year of movement]. For this is approximately those ages x exact at the 31 December in the middle of the year of movement or $x + \frac{1}{2}$ exact (x last birthday) at the end of the year of movement.

Population Projections

In making forward as distinct from current estimat/ tion the term 'projection' is used, rather than 'fore/ is an important one. Demographers can do no more existing trends of births, deaths, migration and throw the... (extrapolate them) into the future. This is a purely mechanical ope.. tion carrying no expectation of fulfilment as would be implied by the term 'forecast'. In projecting existing trends we are doing no more than spell out these implications in terms of what must happen if these trends are maintained. There is no implication that they *will* be maintained. Indeed there is often an expectation that they will not be maintained. Trends do change, sometimes quite suddenly as when births began to rise steeply in this country in 1955 and when they began to fall in 1965. Sometimes the projections (the implications of existing trends) stimulate action which alters the trends. There is no doubt that the publicity given to the effect of continuing rapid population growth in the less developed areas has stimulated in a number of countries (India, Pakistan, United Arab Republic, Taiwan, for example) the institution of official population policies aimed at restricting growth. Conversely the virtual cessation of growth in the population of France in the late 1930's, when deaths actually exceeded births, led to drastic economic measures to encourage fertility. Projections soon become out-of-date therefore and have to be regularly revised to take account of changes in the underlying trends. Sometimes the need for revision is based not so much on changes in trends as improved information of these trends. In England and Wales information about migration is still scanty (p. 107) and the available data on fertility (p. 53) though substantial is not such as to permit analyses of motivation towards, and intentions about, family planning which would permit surer assumptions to be made about long term trends. There is therefore always scope for sharper definition of trends and, on these grounds alone, a new look at the projection.

Method

The basic method is the same as that used for intercensal estimates except that the components of the calculation are not actual but future events. In the following formulae, the *prefix* relates to the *calendar* year and the *suffix* relates to *age* last birthday.

The calculation moves forward from year to year separately for each sex and for each single year of age by the formula.

$$^{n}p_x = {}^{n-1}p_{x-1}(1 - {}^{n-1}q_{x-\frac{1}{2}}) + {}^{n}M_x$$

where $^n p_x$ = number of persons at mid-year n aged x last birthday

$^n M_x$ = net migrants inward (if outward, it becomes a negative quantity) in the period mid-year $n - 1$ to mid-year n, aged x last birthday at mid-year n

$^{n-1} q_{x-\frac{1}{2}}$ = probability of death within a year for a person aged $(x - 1)$ last birthday at mid-year $n - 1$.

It is usual to ignore the mortality of migrants between the date of migration and mid-year n.

At age 0 the formula is

$$^n p_0 = {}^n B (1 - {}^{n-\frac{1}{2}} q_0) + {}^n M_0$$

where $^n B$ = number of live births in period mid-year $n - 1$ to mid-year n

$^{n-\frac{1}{2}} q_0$ = probability that a baby born in the period mid-year $n - 1$ to mid-year n will die before the end of that period.

Base Population

This will be the latest available mid-year estimate of the *total* population (for the same reason as given above in relation to inter-censal estimates).

Mortality

It will be clear that a forecast has to be made of $^n q_x$ applicable to some year in the future. Age rates of mortality tend, despite the apparently dramatic nature of medical advances, to move fairly steadily and their extrapolation either by graphic representation or the assumption of a mathematical law of decrease (e.g. logarithmic) presents little difficulty. There are some constraints. Where rates of mortality have been falling sharply, as for example at young ages in developing countries it may be necessary to regard this as a 'catching up' process and to make some allowance for eventual alignment with trends in developed countries. Where, as at older ages for men in this country, the trend has been level or even upward, it is for consideration, subject to medical advice, whether some ulti-mate improvement may be safely assumed.

Fertility

The estimation of a series of annual numbers of births in the future is itself strictly a component calculation

$$^n B = [\Sigma^n P_x^{mw} . i_x^{mw}] . (1 + k)$$

where mw stands for married women, i for the fertility rate (live births per unit of population, in this case married women) and k is an allowance for births to unmarried women.

In turn this would mean projecting P_x^{mw} from year to year. This would involve the consideration of marriage, divorce, and remarriage rates and of the marital status of migrants, i.e.

$$_nP_x^{wm} = {}^{n-1}P_{x-1}^{mw}(1 - {}^{n-1}q_{x-\frac{1}{2}}^{mw} - {}^{n-1}d_{x-\frac{1}{2}}^{mw} - {}^{n-1}q_{y-\frac{1}{2}}^{mm})$$
$$+ ({}^{n-1}P_{x-1}^{dw} + {}^{n-1}P_{x-1}^{ww}) \, . \, rm_{x-\frac{1}{2}}$$

where ${}^{n-1}d_{x-\frac{1}{2}}^{mw}$ is the probability of divorce within a year of a married woman aged $(x - 1)$ last birthday at mid-year $n - 1$; ${}^{n-1}q_{y-\frac{1}{2}}^{mm}$ is the probability of death within a year of a husband aged $y - 1$, the average age of husbands of wives aged $x - 1$; ${}^{n-1}P_{x-1}^{dw}$ relates to divorced women; ${}^{n-1}P_{x-1}^{ww}$ relates to widowed women; and $rm_{x-\frac{1}{2}}$ is the probability of remarriage within a year of a divorced or widowed woman aged $(x - 1)$ last birthday at mid-year $n - 1$. This is not all; there would be correction terms dealing for example with the fact that a woman cannot be divorced if she dies first.

The whole operation, including the estimation of births ought to be carried out with reference to age at marriage, so that fertility rates specific for age and duration of marriage can be applied.

It is usual to eschew this degree of refinement and complication which is not appropriate to such a speculative process as population projection. The elements of the calculation are examined in order to form a judgment about the trend in the total flow of births but they are not brought into an integrated calculation.

In the official projections of England and Wales the examination is carried out in the following stages for the first fifteen years of the projection period (usually forty years):

(A) Births on the assumption of no migration after the starting date of the projections

    (i) to women married once only
    (ii) to remarried women
    (iii) to unmarried women

(B) Effect of assumed net migration

For (A) (i) it is necessary to estimate the female population at annual intervals for 15 years by marital status and for married women by age at marriage and duration of marriage. This itself involves a number of stages:

(a) examination of trend of marriage rates

5

(*b*) derivation of expected proportions married by age last birthday in each future year and therefore of spinster populations

(*c*) Estimates of numbers of marriages of spinsters in successive years, by age at marriage (maintaining consistency with effect of bachelors' marriage rate trends)

(*d*) Derivation from (*c*) and records of past marriages of an analysis of married women by age at marriage and duration of marriage, for any year in the 15 years. For example the women married once only of age at marriage 25 and duration of marriage 10 years, in year n will be the survivors of spinsters married at 25 in year $n - 10$ (i.e. of the results of applying the spinster marriage rate at age 25 to the population of spinsters aged 25 in year $n - 10$) with allowance for the relatively small numbers of deaths, widowhoods and divorces, subsequently occurring.

To this population matrix (we use the term to describe a large cross-tabulation of numbers of women by age at marriage and marriage duration for each calendar year) we apply a matrix of fertility rates specific for age at marriage and marriage duration for each calendar year to generate the expected births in each calendar year. In deriving these fertility rates it is usual to have regard to the most stable of all fertility indicators—mean ultimate family size (p. 62); to extrapolate this (by year of marriage) after taking account of likely changes in the factors affecting fertility (changes in level of living, changes in extent of use and efficiency of contraceptive methods) and the results of any population surveys that may have been carried out to gauge the fertility intentions of couples in the early stages of family building; and to adjust the current pattern of age-duration-specific fertility rates to be consistent with the projected mean ultimate family size figures.

The mean ultimate family size for a particular *year* of marriage is the result of adding together the rates in the diagonal of a table of fertility rates (live births per married woman) by marriage duration and calendar year of attaining that duration: for example, for age at marriage 20 and year of marriage 1945 (the figures are hypothetical) see Table Sixteen.

This adjustment is usually effected proportionately over the whole table unless there is clear evidence of a change in the pattern of rates, for example further concentration of family building into the early years of marriage, involving an increase in rates at early marriage durations and a decrease at later durations. In the latter event the adjustment of rates to a particular family size would be a matter of judgment.

Where the diagonals for future years of the type of tabulation shown above have been adjusted to yield the expected family sizes, the horizontal lines of the table (as illustrated for 1970) form the set of rates to be applied to the population in 1970 of women

TABLE SIXTEEN

Fertility rates by duration of marriage and year of experience

Age at marriage	Year of attaining duration	Duration of marriage											
		0	1	2	3	4	5	6	7	8	9	10 etc.	
20	1945	.31											
	1946		.29										
	1947			.28									
	1948				.27								
	1949					.25							
	1950						.23						
	1951							.20					
	1952								.16				
	1953									.13			
	1954										.10		
	1955											.08	
	etc.												
	1970	.33	.31	.30	.28	.26	.23	.20	.15	.12	.09	.07	2.45
	Total (diagonal, over all durations for year of marriage 1945)												2.40

married for the first time at age 20, to yield expected births, for item (A) (i) referred to above.

It is usual to work in groups of marriage ages, for example, under 20, 20–24, 25–29, etc., to cut down the amount of detail.

Item (A) (ii) the births to remarried women would probably be a round figure addition (in England and Wales about 20,000 a year) having regard to the recent run of annual births in this population segment.

The allowance for illegitimate births (item (A) (iii)) is normally a percentage addition of legitimate births based on current experience (in England and Wales, about 7–8 per cent).

As to the special fertility allowance for migrants (item (B)) we have to remember that they are included in (A) so that the only consideration is whether they bring with them any substantial fertility differential. Migrants from less developed areas usually have higher fertility on arrival than those of the receiving country if that country is economically developed as is commonly the case; it is also usual for their descendants to assimilate the family size attitudes of the population into which they are born. It is therefore necessary, if there has been a large influx of such migrants, to quantify

5A

that influx in terms of women in the fertile age groups in successive years and to allow for their fertility being initially fifty per cent (say) higher than the indigenous female population, the loading being assumed to decrease as time passes. Although item (B) may be significant and not to be ignored it is likely to be small relative to (A), and very approximate methods would be adequate to estimate the future annual addition to births from the differential fertility of migrants. Official projections for England and Wales for 1980 made in 1964 allowed for an addition of 23,000 live births against an original total (without this allowance) of 961,000.

Migration

The balance of migration is an element liable to considerable variation from year to year as a result of changes in world economic conditions or political decisions by Governments. It is necessary to make a judgment as to the annual figure which, over the longer run, is likely to represent average conditions. This figure has then to be distributed by sex and age on the basis of recent experience (see p. 116).

REFERENCES

The Quarterly Return of the General Register Office for March of any year contains statements of methods and results of official national projections.

Schneider, J. R. L. *Local Population Projections in England and Wales*, Population Studies 10, 95 (1956).

Thompson, E. J. *Population Projections for the South-east*, Studies on Medical and Population Subjects No. 21. General Register Office (1967).

Proceedings of the World Population Conference 1965, Volume III. United Nations (1967). (Contains papers on projections and population trends.)

10

Sickness measurement

SICKNESS and health are antitheses and are difficult to define except in terms of each other. A morbid condition is a departure from the normal healthy condition, and the prevalence of disease can only be assessed given adequate and practical criteria for defining departure from normality. Death is a clearly determinable event. Sickness is not such an event but a state somewhere between health and death and its identification depends upon both the criteria used and the type of observer applying them. The aim of this chapter is to review some of the problems and techniques that have arisen in the different modes of measurement of sickness applicable to different definitions of ill-health, and to different agencies identifying the ill-health. Apart from the varying standards of health and diagnosis involved there are a number of different unitary concepts involved. Illness is a condition which continues for a period of time. We may, therefore, consider how many sickness periods (illnesses) began in a specified interval or how many terminated during the interval or how many were current at any time during the interval. We have also to distinguish between persons and illnesses, remembering that a person can have more than one illness within an interval and even at the same point of time. An illness may be a new disease or a recurrence of a disease suffered on some previous occasion. An attempt will be made to define the units used on every occasion; in general, the term 'incidence' will relate to the emergence of new cases (a 'flow' concept) and 'prevalence' to the numbers existing at a point of time (a 'stock' concept).

NORMALITY

In considering what is ill-health we are confronted with a wide range of variability between one individual and another in every structure and function of the human body. There is no unique pattern of structure or of behaviour to which all living members must conform, but a whole distribution of bodily structures and functions which are equally 'healthy' in the sense of absence of any observable impediment to existence.

Many clinical errors have arisen from failure to recognize the normal range of variability. The palpability of epitrochlear glands which is present in forty per cent of adult males was once regarded as a symptom of disease, particularly of syphilis. Myotatic irritability of the pectoral muscles commonly present in healthy individuals (a form of the familiar stretch reflex) was often referred to as a suggestive sign of pulomonary tuberculosis or other debilitating disease. Von Graafe's sign (lid lag) was once thought to be peculiar to thyrotoxicosis, but it is now known to be present in other diseases, especially peptic ulcer, and it has no diagnostic value in relation to its hyperthyroid connexions. A significant proportion of fit young men exhibit a degree of gastric acidity which at one time would have been regarded as pathological and suggestive of duodenal ulceration. In 1946 there was published a survey of a group of young students at Harvard 'who had general all-round "normal" reactions'. The following are some of the medical data:

Measurement	No. of individuals	Mean	Range
Pulse: recumbent	259	66·1	40·0 – 96·0
Blood pressure, recumbent (mm. of Hg):			
Systolic	265	114·9	98·0 –146·0
Diastolic	265	71·7	40·0 – 92·0
Red blood cells (millions/cu.m.m.)	254	5·04	4·25– 5·60
Haemoglobin (%)	255	97·4	85·4 –107·8
Blood sugar (mg. %)	147	100·0	84·0 –125·0
Respiratory ventilation (l./min.)	209	7·0	3·5 – 14·4

Though blood pressure tends to rise with advancing age it is difficult to say when this is pathological, even though safety margins may be reduced. Hobson and Pemberton found that in a random sample of old people living at home forty-three per cent had a resting diastolic blood pressure of 100 mm. of mercury or over and most of these were 'in good health'. Blood pressures fitted a Normal curve and the dispersion as indicated by the mean ± twice the standard deviation was (mm. of Hg):

	Males	Females
Systolic	107·3–236·9	117·4–250·6
Diastolic	55·4–127·4	66·2–131·8

There was no significant correlation between height of the systolic or diastolic blood pressure and any symptom of disease or absence of well-being.

The human eye provides an interesting example of successful correlation between elements which vary freely over quite a wide range; though the various components of the optic system (axial length, depth of anterior chamber, refractive power of lens, refractive power of cornea) are each distributed Normally in the population, the distribution of total optical refraction is not Normal but is very sharply peaked—the long eye tends to get a thin cornea and lens.

ABNORMALITY

It is the successful adaptation of the complex human organism as a whole to the particular variates of composition and function with which it is endowed and to the external environment in which it has to survive that constitutes good health. Account must also be taken of the need to adapt to physical and emotional stresses, and to environmental changes. This adaptation is essential to stability and survival, but it is not satisfactory to measure sickness simply by failure to survive, though in the last resort, for example in underdeveloped countries where morbidity statistics are deficient, mortality may be used as an index of general health.

COMMUNICABLE DISEASE

It was in fact the danger to other persons as well as to the patient that stimulated the earliest form of morbidity reporting, i.e. statutory notification of infectious disease; and it was the spread of 'fearful diseases overstepping the locality where they are born' with which early epidemiologists were concerned.

The purposes of notification cover

(a) Planning of facilities for treatment, for example opening up of a pool of hospital beds when necessary
(b) Local administrative action

   (i) isolation of infectious cases or sources of infection
   (ii) prophylaxis
   (iii) disinfection
   (iv) after-care

(c) Medical intelligence

   (i) epidemic control
   (ii) morbidity indices

(d) Epidemiological research
(e) Diagnostic study

Morbidity measurement is only one and not the most important of many objectives, most of which are concerned with action in the field of medical administration.

The following diseases are notifiable in England and Wales: anthrax, cholera, diphtheria, dysentery, encephalitis, erysipelas, food poisoning, leprosy, malaria, measles, meningococcal infection, plague, pneumonia, poliomyelitis, puerperal pyrexia, scabies, small-pox, tuberculosis, typhoid fever, typhus, whooping cough. Many of these diseases have been virtually banished from this country by modern hygiene—anthrax, cholera, leprosy, malaria, plague, small-pox, typhoid, typhus—and the incidence of diphtheria has been dramatically reduced, by measures of immunization, to an insignificant level. Antibiotics and sulpha drugs have so added to the efficacy of treatment that dysentery, erysipelas, measles, pneumonia, puerperal pyrexia and whooping cough have ceased to be regarded as dangerous in the absence of any specially complicating factors such as pre-existing disease or advanced age.

The normal method of measurement of incidence is to express new cases notified within a specified interval as a rate per 1,000 of the population at risk. Where infectious diseases are endemic it is merely a matter of time before the infection is encountered, and since the period of time is short the common fevers are characteristically diseases of childhood; for this reason the population at risk is sometimes restricted to those under age 15, though detailed treatment usually extends to the provision of rates for at least ages 0–4, 5–9, 10–14, 15–24, 25–44, 45 and over. A useful summary measurement is obtained by ignoring mortality and assessing the risk of contracting the disease before age y by the expression

$$\sum_{x=0}^{x=y-t} t \cdot r_{x/x+t-1}$$

where $r_{x/x+t-1}$ is notification rate for the age group x to $x + t$ calculated over a period sufficiently long to embrace the normal proportion of epidemic and non-epidemic years. For measles which in most large towns is epidemic in alternate years a two-year period is sufficient; for whooping cough and scarlet fever there is no fixed epidemic rhythm, though there is considerable variation in incidence from year to year, and it is advisable to take a period of two or three years.

For infectious disease to be notifiable it has to be recognized, which usually means that there have to be overt symptoms. An intriguing problem of modern epidemiology is provided by the subclinical (symptomless) infection which appears to be a necessary postulate to explain the epidemic behaviour of at least two diseases, measles and poliomyelitis.

Epidemiological research has been much stimulated by the application of modern probability theory. The classical mathematical models have been deterministic in the sense that given rates of infection and accession and removal of susceptibles, the number of new cases arising in a particular interval of time is definite and determined by the proportion of the population which is still susceptible at that time. This leads to an epidemic curve of the type

$$x = m + \int_0^t (a - z) \, \mathrm{d}t \quad \text{or} \quad \frac{\mathrm{d}x}{\mathrm{d}t} = a - z$$

where z = cases per unit time, x = number of susceptibles, a = accessions of susceptibles per unit time, m = steady state, or level, number of susceptibles, when one infects one.

A more complete stochastic model should, however, be used to take account of the fact that the single point on the deterministic curve ought to be regarded as the mean of a probability distribution. The smoothness of observed epidemics which has seemed to support deterministic theory arises from the fact that the statistics observed represent combinations of several restricted epidemics occurring at the same time with attack rates further smoothed by being averaged over finite intervals. Nevertheless, while the deterministic curves indicate the growth of an epidemic when numbers are large, they are not adequate when numbers are small or in the important early stages of an epidemic. The mathematics of the stochastic approach are formidable and lead to equations which are far from simple, but they appear to offer a sounder basis for prediction. One practical advantage may be mentioned. The deterministic theory involved a degree of damping in successive epidemic waves which is not observed in large communities. The stochastic theory does not result in damping terms in the equations and permits recapitulation of epidemic waves more in accord with experience.

TUBERCULOSIS

Tuberculosis has been so grave a problem in itself that it has always been considered apart from other infectious diseases. First of all there is a contrast between infection and disease; a large proportion of the population are infected before or during adolescence and there are comparatively few adults who have not had a history of infection, whereas the proportion of the population on the registers of tuberculous patients supervised by chest clinics is less than one per cent.

Thus only a small proportion of those infected ever show significant signs of disease—the majority of primary infections heal uneventfully without active treatment. Secondly, the disease is characterized by a long period of chronic invalidity; even before chemotherapeutic agents were used the average period between notification and death for respiratory tuberculosis was two years and the deaths were fairly widely dispersed in time. Since the introduction of streptomycin and other antibiotic and chemotherapeutic agents and the bolder lung surgery which the powerful antibiotic 'covers' have permitted, mortality from tuberculosis has plunged downward. Much longer periods of survival are now involved. Even though results of treatment are infinitely better now than formerly it is clear that the disease prevents the sufferer from carrying on a normal life for a period of a year or so in most cases, and in some cases for years.

Since the disease spread throughout the community each succeeding generation has fared better in combating the ravages of the 'white scourge'. This feature has been extensively analysed on a cohort mortality basis. Generally the results may be summarized by saying that though for men the secular trend is that the peak of mortality in middle adult life has moved steadily to later ages and become diminished, this is mainly due to succeeding generations having lower mortality, so that the residual (at late ages) of the high mortality of an early cohort is greater than the early adult peak of the present generation; for women in whom the disease has always been more fulminating and less chronic the peak has remained in early adult life but has become greatly diminished. This has led to the suggestions that more developed communities have been 'breeding out' the disease (i.e. producing, by natural selection, genetic strains of lessened susceptibility), or alternatively, that the bacillus itself has become less virulent. There is little evidence to support either suggestion. A much simpler explanation is possible. The problem of tuberculosis is a volumetric problem of a reservoir of infection, i.e. of the quantity of bacilli freely circulating. Reducing the spread of the disease both by isolating diagnosed infectors or reducing their infectiousness by treatment and also by providing fewer opportunities for unknown infectors to infect others in crowded and ill-ventilated workshops, and increasing general resistance to disease by improved social conditions, has resulted in succeeding generations having a reduced risk of meeting heavy doses of bacilli. This process has been tremendously accelerated by the great rapidity with which modern chemotherapy sterilizes the lesion and renders the patient non-infectious, and by improved case-finding which has enabled more infectors to be detected and rendered non-infectious. It should be borne in mind that it is indeed a question of how much disease is contracted in early adult life, as most of the morbidity of later adult life is due to breakdown of old lesions. The risk of contracting disease in adolescence is clearly diminishing.

CANCER REGISTRATION

Another way in which sickness may be identified is in the form of a system of total registration of cases of malignant disease. Where disease runs a long chronic course, something more than mere notification is required. Treatment is protracted; in some cases radical and in others palliative. There exists, at any one time, a large population of patients in various stages of the disease. In the absence of a specific cure of unquestioned efficacy there is at any one time not only a large volume of treatment in process but also a large programme of research into new forms of therapy. There is a great need for information of aetiological significance, of response to treatment and of ultimate survival, for different sites and stages of disease, for different methods of treatment and for different sections of the population; and this information must be on a comparable, i.e. uniform, basis. A system of registration existed in this country before World War II for cases treated by radiotherapy as part of the control over radium, an expensive commodity; this was reorganized by the Radium Commission in 1945 in accordance with Ministry of Health and General Register Office proposals, and in 1947 the General Register Office took responsibility for the operation of the system. When the National Health Service Act came into effect in 1948 the continuation and extension of the plan for cancer records became the responsibility of the integrated hospital service. Though registration is not compulsory there is a gradual approach to completeness; in some areas this has almost been reached, though over the country as a whole it is doubtful whether more than two-thirds of all malignant cases are registered.

Common measures are the survival and recovery rates as defined in Table Seventeen. The correction of the survival rate for 'normal' survival introduces the need for considering life tables omitting the operation of a particular cause—in this case cancer.

Something must be said about cancer of the lung, the increase in the mortality from which in older men has, with arterio-sclerotic heart disease, overshadowed improvements in mortality from other causes such as tuberculosis. Atmospheric pollution is a factor but a more important association between smoking (especially cigarette smoking) and lung cancer mortality has been established. In such vitally important aetiological studies the 'longitudinal' study, viz.

TABLE SEVENTEEN
Cancer, measures of survival and recovery

Definitions	Rate	Crude	Adjusted
Period = either from date of commencement of treatment or from first diagnosis but must be stated	Survival rate: number of persons alive at end of period of observation as proportion of those alive at beginning	$SR_{cru} = \dfrac{A}{A+D+L}$	$SR_{cor} = \dfrac{SR_{cru}}{p}$ to allow for natural mortality
A = alive at end of period A_0 = no evidence of disease A_c = cancer present A_x = presence of cancer uncertain	Apparent recovery rate: number alive with no evidence of disease as a proportion of those alive at beginning of period of observation	$RR_{cru} = \dfrac{A_0}{A+D+L}$	$RR_{adj} = \dfrac{A_0\left[1+\dfrac{A_x}{A_0+A_c}\right] + \tfrac{1}{2}D_0\left[1+\dfrac{D_x+L}{D_0+D_c}\right]}{A+D+L}$
D = known to be dead (similar suffixes apply to conditions at death as for A)			to allow for period of freedom of disease of deaths and untraced. Other possibilities are to equate D_x to zero and to omit L altogether
L = untraced at end of period			
p = survival rate (comparable for age, etc.) in general population excluding cancer			

following up well-defined groups forward in time, is clearly to be preferred to retrospective methods.

PRIVATE INSURANCE RECORDS

Coronary heart disease has been mentioned, and this provides an example of another method of sickness identification, the use of private sickness insurance records. The now classic study of coronary heart disease in male medical practitioners of Morris, Heady and Barley (1952) was based on the sickness and death records of 6,000 members of an assurance society, aged thirty-five to sixty-four, who held non-cancellable sickness insurance, providing benefit, on receipt of a medical certificate, for periods of incapacity to work which lasted seven days or more. The following statistics were derived:

(a) The annual incidence (by age) of first clinical attacks of coronary heart disease (coronary thrombosis, acute myocardial infarction and angina pectoris) during 1947–50.

(b) The annual death-rate in the period from this cause, subdivided not only by age but according to whether death occurred in the first six days of the first clinical attack, in the remainder of the first month, or later.

(c) The prevalence of coronary heart disease in 1950, i.e. the total proportion disabled from work during the year for as much as a week, or dying. It was also possible to give a measure of those attacked in 1949–50 who were not disabled in 1950.

(d) The prognosis for life, i.e. chance of survival for specified periods of time up to seven years from first attack.

(e) The prognosis for further sickness absence, i.e. proportion absent again within a specified period of time and total working time lost.

(f) Comparisons were made of the separate experiences of general practitioners, general practitioner-specialists, full-time consultants and medical administrators, and comparisons were made with a large miscellaneous group of men in the civil services, in the professions and industry.

This study is of especial interest in that life-table techniques were extensively used both in the derivation of the desired rates (it was, for example, necessary to consider separately the decrements of deaths from coronary heart disease and deaths from all other causes) and in presentation of the results.

SOCIAL INSURANCE AND SICKNESS ABSENCE RECORDS

While private insurance records alone lend themselves to detailed analysis there is a great deal of information about morbidity from

National Insurance records. At first sight absence from work or (if not employed) inability to participate in the daily activities normally undertaken, appeals as a clear and unequivocal indication of sickness and on the whole this is true but there are two important reservations:

(a) Sickness absence for employed persons is often associated not only with the payment of National Insurance benefit but with benefits from private insurance with a Friendly Society and in many cases with maintenance of part or full wages by the employer. The point of time at which an employed person 'goes sick' may depend not only on the absolute fact of feeling unwell but on whether there is any loss of income involved and, if so, upon the degree of incapacity at which any financial pressure to remain at work ceases to operate. The same factors operate to determine the point of time at which he returns to work. Sickness absence becomes therefore a relative measure and may mean different degrees of illness for different groups of workers. Even for non-employed persons a similar difficulty arises; a housewife with a large family and unable to afford assistance may struggle to carry on longer than those with less responsibility and more domestic help.

(b) Not all sickness absence is medically certified, and even where it is so certified the administrative arrangements for the disbursement of sick pay may mean that the medical certificates cannot be made directly available to those who are concerned with statistical analysis, and the quality of the data may suffer in this respect if recording has to be left to works officials whose interests are naturally more in factory administration than in medical statistics and who do not appreciate the problem of classifying diagnoses. Furthermore, the need to submit the medical certificate to an employer may tend to make the medical practitioner circumspect in his description of the condition causing incapacity, if only that in the interests of the patient he may have to give a provisional diagnosis before he is certain (which means that subsequent certificates for the same absence may bear different diagnoses as he becomes more certain) or he may consider it expedient so to word his certificate as to be least likely to jeopardize the continued employment of the patient. Persons not gainfully employed, for example housewives, are less likely to consult doctors for minor degrees of incapacity, and even where the conditions are serious it is unlikely that they would voluntarily produce medical certificates to satisfy the needs of any survey of incapacity; such surveys therefore are only likely to elicit information about the conditions they 'complain' of rather than precise diagnoses. (This is not to say that statistics of 'complaints' are without value.) Generally, therefore, practical conditions militate to weaken the validity of the diagnostic classification of sickness absence records.

Sickness benefit provided by insurance has always been strictly associated with suspension of earning capacity attributable to disability, and has not been primarily concerned with the underlying cause of the disability itself. In these circumstances the establishment of medical diagnosis is less important than the practical difficulty of establishing loss of earning capacity, with the immediate problem of deciding whether inability to work is to be assessed in relation to usual occupation, any alternative employment which might normally be available, or on more absolute standards. The danger of confusing this concept with true morbidity can be emphasized by the fact that even in times of improving hygiene and falling mortality, sickness claims were often found to increase substantially if economic incentive to claim were provided by unemployment or by any relaxation of the rules of the Friendly Societies. From the earliest times therefore the actuary concerned with sickness insurance has been accustomed to measure sickness in terms of the 'average number of weeks of sickness (claim) experienced by each individual between ages x and $x + 1$'.

We are not directly concerned here with the financial aspects of such sickness rates but with information that may be yielded on medical causes of disability. A detailed breakdown of National Insurance statistics is given in the Digest of Statistics Analysing Certificates of Incapacity which is produced regularly by the Ministry of Social Security. Over and above the range of statistics of claims familiar to most actuaries the main interest in the Digest lies in the extensive analysis of spells of sickness by certified medical diagnosis and by duration. With all reservations this is an important source of information on morbidity.

In keeping with this type of information are the sickness absence records maintained by certain of the larger industrial concerns in this country. The recording and classification of diagnoses in sickness absence in industry is a special problem. The type of detailed analysis that would be appropriate to clinical records in hospital or in cause of death classification would not be supported either by the quality of the data or by the use to which the tabulations are put. Broader categories have to be devised, and this cannot be done unless there is some understanding of what a diagnosis means. We are concerned with disability in the context of the particular industrial conditions and with the relationship of changes in those conditions to the production of disability.

SOCIAL SURVEY

From 1944 to 1952 the Social Survey interviewed at the beginning of each month samples of the civilian population of ages sixteen and over and recorded the illnesses and injuries said to have been experienced during each of the two calendar months preceding. The size of each monthly sample throughout England and Wales was about 3,000; it was drawn from local card indexes of the National Register and was representative of all areas, urban and rural. An account of some of the results of this survey has been given by Stocks (1949), and routine tables were published in the Quarterly Returns of the Registrar General from 1947 up to the end of the survey. Stocks tested the adequacy of the sample and found it sufficiently representative and large to support the calculation of incapacity rates by diagnostic group and by age and sex and for quarter to quarter comparisons of sickness incidence. He also examined the 'memory factor', i.e. the tendency for people to post-date the inception of an illness to a date nearer the date of interview or to forget the more remote illnesses. For 'new and recurrent illness starting' the rate (all ages combined) in the more recent month of the interview period was 109 per cent of that for the two months combined for males, and 107 per cent for females; hence the decision to base rates on the two months combined. Several different rates were calculated for routine publication, e.g.:

Prevalence rate, i.e. number of illnesses present in the population at any time during the period, regardless of when they began, per stated number of population.

Sickness rate, i.e. number of persons who were ill at any time during the period, regardless of when they began to be ill, per stated number of population.

Inception rate, i.e. number of illnesses which began during the period, per stated number of population.

Incapacity rate, i.e. total days of incapacity (away from work, or for those not working prevented by illness from going out of doors) per stated number of the population during the period.

Rates were calculated in denary age groups for each sex for different medical cause groups, and for all causes combined for different industrial groups and for different income groups (i.e. income of the principal wage earner in the family). Frequency rates of medical consultation were also recorded. The survey of sickness provided a general indication of the level of morbidity in the population at a time when other sources of information were not developed. A possible criticism of the survey is that general statements of symptoms by the public themselves were forced into a detailed diagnostic classification, whereas the sickness presented here was essentially a record of how people 'felt'. Indeed, a survey of 'complaints' related strictly to what the people interviewed actually said would provide a valuable supplement to analyses of medically certified sickness; it might help to provide a bridge between vague symptomology (backache, depression, etc.) and identifiable anatomical or physiological abnormality.

HOSPITAL RECORDS

A possible method of identifying sickness (of a severer character) is by reference to hospital admission. The advantage is that in most cases a firm diagnosis can be made, supported by every available objective clinical and laboratory test, and a clear description given of treatment. There are, however, serious disadvantages. Morbidity implies a risk or rate, and there is no population at risk to which tabulations of hospital clinical records can be related until 'catchment areas' can be more precisely defined. Furthermore, inquiries based on in-patient records are directed, not to all sickness, nor to all sickness serious enough to be treated in hospital, but only to those illnesses which in the circumstances of the moment (waiting lists, medical priorities, etc.) are actually accepted for hospital treatment. Unless patients can be compelled to utilize a particular hospital rather than one of choice, and unless hospitals are equally compelled to accept a rigidly defined spread of diseases and degrees of severity, these disadvantages appear likely to continue.

This is not to say that hospital records are not a valuable source of information about the actual utilization of hospitals, and forms and results of treatment. The principal value of hospital in-patient analyses lies in the picture they present of the contemporary clinical work undertaken by the individual hospital. Changes in this picture over a period of time provide information which is essential to the proper allocation of beds, surgical facilities, ancillary diagnostic services and staff; to the arrangement of teaching programmes; to the design of selective admission policy. Statistics of outcome of treatment (recovery rates, incidence of complications, length of stay) for specific diagnostic entities can provide an index of the efficacy of hospital care. All this is essential but it is not morbidity measurement.

There are exceptions to all sweeping assertions. A number of acute forms of disease are invariably admitted to hospital, for example some acute fevers (tuberculous meningitis, poliomyelitis, typhoid, diphtheria, meningococcal infection, etc.), acute psychosis, abdominal emergencies (acute appendicitis, perforated peptic ulcer, obstructed hernia), renal or urinary calculus, osteomyelitis, major injuries, burns and poisonings. For such conditions as these it would be true to say that national hospital admission rates could be calculated and an assessment made of age, sex and occupational differentials.

GENERAL PRACTITIONER RECORDS

Most medical care services have their focus in the family doctor, and it is natural to look to general practitioner records for comprehensive statistics of morbidity. Ideally the general practitioner would be making regular observation of families within his care and noting the incipience of the earliest symptoms of even minor degrees of disease. This ideal is some distance away. Owing to freedom of choice the general practitioner does not see all members of the family, except in a proportion of cases as low as sixty per cent for the typical family of a married couple with children, and since practices are large he does not see them regularly but only when they are sufficiently unwell to demand his attention.

A further difficulty is that general practitioner records by their very nature do not lend themselves easily to statistical analysis. When a patient enters the surgery of a general practitioner it is by no means usual for an immediate diagnosis to be made; if it were so it might simplify statistical analysis but it would probably not be good medicine. Very often the record card of a patient will show a series of visits with notes of various symptoms and reaction to prescribed treatment, and the patient may then be referred to hospital without a formal diagnosis necessarily being recorded (though most hospitals now endeavour to keep general practitioners fully informed about the progress of patients referred to consultants), or alleviation of symptoms may cut short attendances and the record may not be completed unless the doctor has the opportunity to review his records for that purpose. Patients sometimes attend for minor degrees of discomfort or for advice, for example, about fitness for jobs or about marriage, and in such cases there may be a great deal observed but little to record. Despite these difficulties a number of important studies of illness in general practice have been made.

The main morbidity measures emerging from general practitioner records are: (1) the rate of new cases of particular disease groups per 1,000 persons registered within a specified interval, by sex and age;

(2) the proportion of persons in a particular sex and age group who consult their doctor t times within a specified interval ($t = 0, 1, 2, \ldots$); (3) frequency distributions of duration of treatment.

A difficulty which has not been entirely solved and which affects the accuracy of populations at risk used as the denominators of rates, is the inflation of doctors' lists arising from the lag in, or omission of, notification of removal. Arrangements exist for the notification of removal on death even where the general practitioner is not in attendance, but in cases of change of practitioner the old list will not normally be corrected until the removing patients register with new doctors, and they may not sign the necessary cards until some ailment brings them to the new doctor's surgery. In the meantime the doctor to whom they transfer has patients actually at risk for whom he has no records, and this helps to offset the inflation due to unnotified removals, but on balance it is found that lists are subject to inflation to an extent which varies according to whether or not a practice is growing.

MENTAL DISORDER

The problem of measuring the total volume of mental disease in the community epitomizes all that has been said about the dispersive character of normality. In a General Register Office survey of general practitioner records it was found that the number of patients consulting their doctors for psychoses, anxiety reaction, asthenic reaction, other psycho-neuroses, alcoholism, mental deficiency and other disorders of character were (annual rates per 1,000 of the practice populations):

Period	Males					Females				
	0–	15–	45–	65+	All ages	0–	15–	45–	65+	All ages
1951–52	15	41	37	34	33	19	77	100	63	68
1952–54	19	40	43	39	34	18	84	98	66	71

These figures are not necessarily representative of the country as a whole, but the rates are impressively large, especially for adult females. Of 4,732 patient consulting for psychoneuroses only 473 or ten per cent were referred to hospital for in-patient or out-patient treatment. Hospital statistics therefore only touch upon the hard core of a very large problem.

It is only in respect of hospital treatment that comprehensive statistics exist. The Ministry of Health compiles statistics based on admission and discharge records of all the National Health Service psychiatric beds in hospitals in England and Wales. The statistics cover age, sex, marital status, occupation, diagnosis, length of stay, cause of death if dying in hospital, and distinguish first admissions from readmission. The broad picture is of a standing mental hospital population fed by admissions tending to be concentrated both in early adult life and at advanced ages, a large proportion of which is subject to rapid turnover with a duration of stay of only a few months and with a hard core remainder who stay for very long periods, in many cases until death.

Community Health Records

A comprehensive measure of sickness requires a comprehensive record of episodes of sickness of the individual in their entirety covering the intervention of all agencies—general practitioner, hospital, local authority health and welfare services, etc.—which may have contact with the individual. All these records are at present separated, though some attempts have been made to bring some of them together by record linkage systems. However the ideal, viz. a single medical record to which can be posted the medical history of an individual as it unfolds, is now attainable as a consequence of the introduction of computers to medicine.

The basis of such a system of community health records already exists in the hospital service where information systems known as 'hospital activity analysis' are being extensively introduced. The hospital is the easiest point at which to begin because the standard of recording and the medical sophistication of records is higher than in other branches of the National Health Service. This sophistication itself compels the introduction of computers so that on grounds of access to facilities for data processing the hospital is the natural focus.

There has to be a basic information system in the hospital to provide a vehicle for the extensive storage of clinical data; an information system into which the various disciplines in the hospital can feed data, and retrieve them, and which, moreover, serves as a means of communication between the disciplines. The computer provides the means to this end.

Hospital activity analysis essentially is a development of those statistical processes already carried on in hospitals to include information about patients, and about the use of care facilities. The immediate management improvement is that this information can be processed by computer, analysed by the statistician, and rapidly fed back to the hospitals in order to provide the administrators, and above all the medical staff committee, with information that will be of direct assistance to them in improving the organization of the hospital.

All hospitals maintain registration procedures, which are initiated by the patient's first contact with the hospital, and which embody the principles of what is known as the unit system. The main object of these procedures is to ensure that the clinician can at any time retrieve from the record library a particular patient's case history which covers all his previous contacts with the hospital, whether the record is referred to by unit number, patient's name, diagnostic entity or surgical operation. For this purpose there are usually manually operated card indexes for the three main axes of classification—number, diagnosis and operation. In addition hospitals maintain waiting lists, admission and discharge registers, and often ancillary statistical records of out-patient attendances and in-patient treatment, even if these records are kept only in ledger form.

The common factor in all this documentation is the patient.The new system telescopes these documentation procedures in such a way that one card or sheet of paper is associated with the patient in all his contacts with the hospital and forms a single vehicle for carrying a summary of all the hospital activity which he generates; this summary sheet is translated on to a punched card for data processing. Given that there is access to data-processing facilities in the hospital, these cards can be processed automatically, replacing both the existing statistical procedures and the manual indexes of diagnoses and operations, so that information about its activity can be given to the hospital on the basis specified by the hospital, and also can be contributed to regional and national surveys.

Information that can be provided in this way for local use includes an analysis of the waiting-list by specialty and by individual consultant, tabulated according to the patient's age and sex, the degree of urgency, and the length of time he has been waiting; summaries can be provided for the use of individual consultants showing the total number of cases treated during a given period, the patients' lengths of stay, the turnover of patients, and how the beds were occupied; figures for preceding periods can also be shown for comparison, and diagnoses can be tabulated.

Given this kind of basic vehicle for information, storage and retrieval, the system can be extended. In the original feedback a minimum uniform content is laid down in order to permit integration to regional and national tabulations and analyses. Above this minimum, encouragement is given to provide the greatest possible local orientation and flexibility—adding things that are locally necessary, for such periods of time as are required to satisfy a need, and then discarding them. The vehicle can then be loaded in a number of different ways:

(a) The addition of more and more clinical material as this becomes effectively documented, and the technical means of input and retrieval become more developed. This will eventually provide rapid reproduction of individual histories and, collectively, a matrix of probabilities linking symptomatology, diagnosis and prognosis as an extension of the human memory, and not as a substitute for judgment. In particular it is likely that, just as there is at present a special part of the total transcript for obstetrics (because the data requirements are special), so there will be special extensions for other types of cases, for example cancer registration could be absorbed in the system; there could be special treatment of radiology and pathology.

(b) As different disciplines in the hospital begin to feed in to the common record they automatically become joined together in better communication, via the information system, with each other.

(c) Better data links will mean more on-line collection and pre-processing of records, for example, parameters of electro-cardiograms.

(d) Cancer registration and other forms of statistical surveillance can be automatic by-products.

(e) Most important, given the adoption of a uniform numbering system for identifying patients, there is no reason why the general practitioner and the medical officer of health should not be connected to the system. This would then provide prospective record linkage, i.e. the data would be posted to a common record at the moment of recording instead of retro-spectively (after records have been created in separate places) as in current systems. The general practitioner, for example, would be able to recall the whole record for diagnostic and therapeutic assistance. This is very important because, unless record linkage provides for feedback, its value is considerably diminished.

In this way there is a natural development to a system of community health records in which the computer, with the general practitioner as the natural focus, joins into one information system the patient and all those who have anything to do with his care. The technological means have been solved to the extent that experimentation has already begun.

At the outset nothing more sophisticated is needed than a relatively simple transcription form for each episode of sickness so that participation by the general practitioner calls for no more than reasonable secretarial assistance. Later one can consider remote input devices for direct communication with the computer. Quite early in the process comprehensive morbidity measurement will have become possible.

REFERENCES

Benjamin, B. *Health and Vital Statistics*. Allen and Unwin, London (1968).

Bradford Hill, A. *Medical Statistics*, 8th edition. Lancet, London (1966).

Measurement of Morbidity. Studies on Medical and Population Subjects No. 8. General Register Office (1954).

Supplement to Statistical Review 1949. General Register Office (1955).

Hobson, W. and Pemberton, J. *The Health of the Elderly at Home*. Butterworths, London (1955).

Morris, J. M., Heady, J. A. and Barley, R. G. *British Medical Journal*, p. 503 (1952).

Stocks, P. *Sickness in the Population of England and Wales 1944–7*. Studies on Medical and Population Subjects No. 2. General Register Office (1949).

Taylor, I. and Knowelden, J. *Principles of Epidemiology*, 2nd edition. J. H. Churchill (1964).

11

Manpower statistics

ECONOMIC planning clearly involves the forecasting of manpower needs not only nationally, industry by industry, but also within individual establishments.

Concepts of stock and of flow are involved. We need to know the present supply (stock) and to compare this with estimated requirements in order to arrive at a measure of imbalance, if any, within any industrial system, whether it be a whole industry, a single production unit, or a specific employment category. This imbalance will not be static but dynamic. There will be 'ageing' effects, future recruitment, wastage (labour mobility) and age retirement. All these are flow elements.

Census Figures

The basic measure of stock is the census; for national purposes the population census and for management purposes within establishments, a census of staff, i.e. a print-out of the up-dated staff register which has to be maintained for pay-roll, pensions and other personnel control purposes. By themselves these figures give some indication of flow elements. For example the age structure of the labour force will clearly reflect the normal ages of recruitment and of retirement. The later the age of recruitment the more likely it is that pre-entry training or experience in some lower grade employment is required, i.e. the entry, to the employment considered, emerges from a longer pipe-line and therefore changes in supply may take longer to effect than for unskilled employment. A new medical school will not increase the supply of doctors until some seven years after its opening. Apart from what may be read into them directly, the census figures have also to serve as denominators for measuring recruitment, wastage and other rates. For all these reasons the census counts must achieve a sufficient degree of specificity and comparability. These are the two methodological points which arise here.

It must be possible to calculate rates specific for sex, age, marital status, occupation, industry, status within occupation (foreman, manager, etc.) and often it will be necessary to classify by duration of service and other factors such as professional qualifications and even previous career characteristics. Whatever the basis of classification of the denominators (the numbers at risk) the same basis must be applied to the numerators of rates (the 'flow' elements) otherwise the rates will be erroneous and even meaningless.

Classification of Occupations and Industries (Branches of Economic Activity)

The classification of occupations most commonly in use is that compiled by the General Register Offices of England and Wales and of Scotland for use in the population census. It is normally revised and reissued as an H.M.S.O. publication ('Classification of Occupations') a year or so before each Census. A more detailed, i.e. more job-content-specific, classification is used for placement purposes by the Ministry of Labour* but this is not intended for statistical purposes and is not used in demographic work. Both classifications are related to (i.e. translatable into) the International Statistical Classification of Occupations compiled by the International Labour Office, international comparability is therefore secured.

There are four separate aspects of the employment or former employment of a person

(a) Economic position (active or inactive)
(b) Employment status (for example self-employed, apprentice, etc.)
(c) Industry (commonly referred to as branch of economic activity)
(d) Occupation

The classification by *economic position* distinguishes first the economically active from the inactive. Among the active we separate family workers (those living in the same household as their employer) from other occupied persons and those out of employment. There is a further division of each of the two occupied groups into full-time and part-time; those out of employment may be split into (a) sick, (b) others. The economically inactive are subdivided into institutional inmates, the retired, students, and others who are inactive. There are a number of important matters of definition which apply especially here and also to the other classifications. First there is a need for a time reference. The question 'are you employed?' naturally evokes the question 'when—today, yesterday, usually, ever?' It is usual therefore to define a point of time (a particular day) or a short period

* Now Ministry of Employment and Productivity.

(for example, the week before the census), to which all the information is related. When is a person *in* employment? It is usual to agree conventionally that those absent on account of strikes, lock-outs, short-time working, sickness (unless employment has actually terminated for this reason) or holidays are to be regarded as in employment.

A mere statement of occupation is not sufficient either to determine level of living or occupational health risk (if any) or training content or job content unless qualified by a statement indicating whether the occupation in the individual case is followed in a supervisory or operational capacity; whether in an employed or an employer capacity. This qualification is classified under the heading of employment status, as follows:

Employment Status

  (*a*) *Self-employed*

      (i) without employees
      (ii) with employees

         (A) large establishments
         (B) small establishments

  (*b*) *Employees*

      (i) Managers

         (A) large establishments
         (B) small establishments

      (ii) Foremen and supervisors

         (A) manual
         (B) non-manual

      (iii) Apprentices, articled pupils, formal trainees
      (iv) Employees (not elsewhere classified)

A self-employed person is one not employed by any person or company and persons working in their own home for an employer (outworkers). Directors of limited companies are excluded from this category. 'Without employees' means without paid assistance other than family workers. A large establishment is one with twenty-five or more persons.

INDUSTRY

Here we are concerned with the *trade* carried on by firms, *not* the *jobs* performed by individuals in the furtherance of that trade.

For all official purposes there is a Standard Industrial Classification which is revised from time to time by an interdepartmental committee. The last issue was in 1958. It conforms, generally, to the International Standard Industrial Classification of all Economic Activities issued by the United Nations.

The classification is based on industries without regard to their nature of ownership or operation. Manufacturing units owned or operated by the Central Government are classified in the same way as those in private hands and are not classified industrially as 'national government service' (government *is* one form of economic activity). Transport services operated by local authorities are likewise included under 'transport' and not under 'local government service'.

The unit of classification is the 'establishment'. This is normally the whole of the premises, such as a farm, a mine, a factory or a shop at a particular address. All activities at that address (including, for example, departments engaged in selling, bottling, packing transport, etc.) are included. There are exceptions. If, at a single address, there are two or more departments engaged in different activities in respect of which separate records are available, each department is treated as a separate establishment.

There are some 150 Minimum List Headings distinguished by arabic numerals (three digits). These Minimum List Headings have been grouped into twenty-four Orders distinguished by roman numerals.

In the actual classification some special points arise.

(a) Merchanting: establishments mainly engaged in merchanting, broking, importing and exporting are classified as in the distributive trades and not in the industry or trade producing the goods for which they are an outlet.

(b) Head office: the head office of a firm operating in the United Kingdom is classified as far as possible according to the major activity of the firm. Head offices of firms trading abroad and carrying on no substantial trading activity in the United Kingdom are assigned to a heading under Miscellaneous Services.

(c) Repair work: where the bulk of the repair work on goods of any particular type is carried out by manufacturers, any establishments specializing in the repair of these goods are assigned to manufacturing. Where most of the repairs are carried out at establishments whose main business is distribution, the specialist repair establishments are also assigned to distribution. For example, establishments repairing radio and television sets, watches and clocks, furniture, etc., are assigned to the distributive trades; those engaged in the repair of ships, locomotives, aircraft, and most kinds of plant and machinery are assigned to manufacturing industry.

Occupation

The 1960 classification contains about 200 unit groups and, subject to the overriding requirements of mortality, morbidity and fertility studies and the preservation of as much comparability as possible with previous classifications, has been based on the International Standard Classification of Occupation, recommended by the International Labour Office[1] for use in National Censuses (it is broadly comparable with the two-digit level of the International Classification).

The basic common factor of all groups is the kind of work done and the nature of the operation performed. But if, by reason of the material worked in, the degree of skill involved, the physical energy required, the environmental conditions, the social and economic status associated with the occupation, or any combination of these factors, unit groups based solely on kind of work were too comprehensive they have been further broken down on the basis of these other factors in order to identify what are substantially separate occupations.

Certain limiting conditions have also operated, for example that the number of individuals likely to be included in a unit is sufficiently large to be worth separate identification, that the identification of a unit group is likely to be tolerably complete and accurate from the limited information obtained from a census, that there is sufficient potential interest in the group to justify separate identification, and that statistics for the group could not be obtained from the cross classifications of occupation by employment status or industry.

The unit groups obtained by the above process have been grouped into orders: these larger groups, like the unit groups, have certain broad features of occupation in common.

Certain groups of persons in employment, in particular the self employed and the managers, give rise to difficult conceptual problems.

Self employed: Even within the same field of economic activity self employed persons range from the working craftsman to the owner and manager of a large industrial concern, extremes for which a single occupational code is not appropriate. But there is no general rule that can be formulated about the size of the undertaking that requires the owner to be occupied mainly on managerial work and,

---

[1] International Labour Office International Standard Classification of Occupations, Geneva 1958.

moreover, especially in mortality and morbidity investigation, the available data affords no indication of the size of undertaking involved. It has been assumed that most self employed persons control or operate only small enterprises, so that they have not been allocated to the managerial group but to an appropriate specific skill. Where self employed persons form an important group whose occupational assignment is not self evident, a specific mention has been made in the occupational unit group concerned. Owners of services, such as typing, office cleaning, car hire, with regard to whom there is no evidence that they perform the actual work associated with such services, are classified as persons *selling* services.

Managers: The growing recognition of management as an occupation in itself, which is to a certain extent independent of the particular field in which it is exercised, has led to managers being classified in a main order of 'administrators and managers'. There are exceptions because in some fields, mainly services, the title of manager is given to persons with comparatively limited responsibilities, and also because in some cases the main activity is that of an occupation other than management. In the first category would come the shop manager and in the second the ship's captain. These persons are given the employment status code of manager but are not coded to the Management Order of the occupation classification.

Professionally and technically qualified persons are classified as managers if an actual charge, at a level above that of works foreman, of the execution of a task either directly or through subordinate managers unless the task so supervised is a professional or technical service.

Foremen: Foremen (other than road and rail transport operating foremen who are classified as supervisors in transport), are classified with the workers they control and distinguished in the status coding.

Labourers: The groups in the classification assigned to labourers are strictly limited to persons performing occupations requiring little or no training or experience and for this reason certain groups of persons who have some degree of skill but are returned as labourers, for example fitter's labourers, are excluded.

Allocation to these groups is on a strictly industrial basis, thus departing from the general basis of classification elsewhere; the industry concerned is that of the 'establishment' taken as a whole.

Apprentices, articled pupils and learners are classified to the group appropriate to those whose training is completed. Graduate and student apprentices are classified to the professional occupation for which they are training.

Armed Forces: For the various economic activity and social

classifications it is intended to keep distinct all uniformed members of the Services, and medical personnel and chaplains are accordingly assigned to the groups for Armed Forces, and not to their professional unit group.

SOCIAL AND SOCIO-ECONOMIC CLASSIFICATIONS

Social Class

Since the 1911 Census it has been customary, as an aid to certain kinds of statistical analysis, to arrange the large number of unit groups of the Occupational Classification into a small number of broad categories (called Social Classes) as follows:

(*a*) Professional, etc., occupations
(*b*) Intermediate occupations
(*c*) Skilled occupations
(*d*) Partly skilled occupations
(*e*) Unskilled occupations

The unit groups included in each of these categories have been selected so as to secure that, so far as is possible, each category is homogeneous in relation to the basic criterion of the general standing within the community of the occupations concerned. This criterion is naturally correlated with (and the application of the criterion conditioned by) other factors such as education and economic environment, but it has no direct relationship to the average level of remuneration of particular occupations. In general each occupational unit group has been assigned as a whole to a Social Class, and it is not a specific assignment of individuals based on the merits of a particular case.

The Social Class appropriate to any combination of occupation and status is derived by the following rules:

(*a*) each occupation is given a basic Social Class
(*b*) persons of foreman status whose basic Social Class is IV or V are allotted to Social Class III
(*c*) persons of manager status are allotted either to Social Class II or III, the latter applying if the basic class is IV or V.

To provide more homogeneous groups, and as a useful alternative axis for classification, Social Classes II, III and IV have been divided into 'manual', 'non-manual', and 'agricultural' sub-groups. Within this framework Social Class I is wholly 'non-manual', Social Class V wholly 'manual'.

Socio-economic Groups

The main criticism of Social Classes has been that because whole occupational unit groups rather than individuals are classified, there is an inherent lack of homogeneity. To meet this, a system of socio-economic groups to which individuals could be assigned was introduced in the 1951 Census. They have since been replaced by somewhat differently derived socio-economic groups based on the census recommendation of the Conference of European Statisticians sponsored jointly by the Statistical Commission and Economic Commission for Europe. The principle is that each socio-economic group should contain people whose social, cultural and recreational standards and behaviour are similar. As it is not practicable to ask direct questions about these subjects in a population census, the allocation of occupied persons to socio-economic groups is determined by considering their employment status and occupation (and industry, though for practical purposes no direct reference is made since it is possible in Great Britain to use classification by occupation as a means of distinguishing effectively those engaged in agriculture).

The socio-economic groups with brief definitions are:

(a) Employers and managers in central and local government, industry, commerce, etc.—large establishments

Persons who employ others or generally plan and supervise in non-agricultural enterprises employing twenty-five or more persons.

(b) Employers and managers in industry, commerce, etc.—small establishments

As in (a) but in establishments employing fewer than twenty-five persons.

(c) Professional workers—self employed

Self employed persons engaged in work normally requiring qualifications of university degree standard.

(d) Professional workers—employees

Employees engaged in work normally requiring qualifications of university degree standard.

(e) Intermediate non-manual workers

Employees, not exercising general planning or supervisory powers, engaged in non-manual occupations ancillary to the professions but not normally requiring qualifications of university degree standard; persons engaged in artistic work and not employing others thereat;

and persons engaged in occupations otherwise included in Group (*f*) who have an additional and formal supervisory function.

(*f*) Junior non-manual workers

Employees, not exercising general planning or supervisory powers, engaged in clerical, sales and non-manual communications and security occupations, excluding those who have additional and formal supervisory functions.

(*g*) Personal service workers

Employees engaged in service occupations caring for food, drink, clothing and other personal needs.

(*h*) Foremen and supervisors—manual

Employees (other than managers) who formally and immediately supervise others engaged in manual occupations, whether or not themselves engaged in such occupations.

(*i*) Skilled manual workers

Employees engaged in manual occupations which require considerable and specific skills.

(*j*) Semi-skilled manual workers

Employees engaged in manual occupations which require slight but specific skills.

(*k*) Unskilled manual workers

Other employees engaged in manual occupations.

(*l*) Own account workers (other than professional)

Self employed persons engaged in any trade, personal service or manual occupation not normally requiring training of university degree standard and having no employees other than family workers.

(*m*) Farmers—employers and managers

Persons who own, rent or manage farms, market gardens or forests, employing people other than family workers in the work of the enterprise.

(*n*) Farmers—own account

Persons who own or rent farms, market gardens or forests and having no employees other than family workers.

(*o*) Agricultural workers

Employees engaged in tending crops, animals, game or forests, or operating agricultural or forestry machinery.

(*p*) Members of Armed Forces

Classification by Size of Establishment

The employers and managers are divided by the size of establishment in which they work to provide some measure of distinction between employers and managers with greater and less responsibility. It is not practicable to ask a question at the census about the degree of responsibility, and in any case there are no clear-cut lines of division or accepted system of classification, but the indirect, rather crude criterion of size of establishment assists towards a distinction. All Civil Service and Local Authority officials coded as managers are conventionally regarded as managers in large establishments.

Measures of Flow

There are a number of related problems of *movement* to be studied in manpower planning. In national economic planning we need to balance the supply and demand for particular occupational groups. There are a number of stages in this process. First the precise job content of the occupation must be established in order to assess the educational restraint on supply, i.e. what period of full-time training must be interposed between leaving school and entry into employment and what period of employment at some lower level of skill or responsibility must further be interposed between initial entry into employment and entry into the occupational group under consideration.

Let us assume for the moment that we know the required annual intake into the occupation, n_x at some modal age x or possibly over a limited distribution of ages, i.e. x takes a number of integral values. This would depend on the normal experience in the occupation. We might, for example, have a situation in which 100,000 are required to enter the occupation at age twenty or alternatively it might be more appropriate to consider an intake of the following character:

Age	No.
19	20,000
20	50,000
21	20,000
22	10,000
	100,000

In some circumstances there might be a much wider spread of entry ages.

The number of school leavers at age sixteen which would be needed to generate this intake, having regard to wastage during the period of full-time or of intermediate employment (if any), has to be calculated. This is a larger number than n_x. To decide how *much* larger, we need to construct a decrement table of the following character (the figures are hypothetical).

Age x (exact)	l_x In intermediate training or employment	w_x^i Withdrawn between x and $x + 1$	d_x^i Died between x and $x + 1$
16	10,000	2,014	8
17	7,978	1,506	10
18	6,462	493	11
19	5,958	364	11
20	5,583		

5,583 at age 20 exact

Thus we need 10,000 school leavers to produce 5,583 entrants to the occupation; or in symbolic terms the required number of school leavers = $n_x . (l_{16}^i / l_{20}^i)$.

The kind of decrement table referred to above (sometimes referred to as a service table) would be calculated from observed rates of mortality and withdrawal. It enables other important relationships to be established apart from the overall wastage from the intermediate training or employment. For example it tells us that a constant annual intake of l_x^i into the intermediate training or employment would produce at any instant a standing intermediate population of $\frac{1}{2}[l_{16}^i + 2l_{17}^i + 2l_{18}^i + 2l_{19}^i + l_{20}^i]$. In our example this would be 28,190. This is the size (stock) of the student population or intermediate labour force.

We may now consider the problem of deriving n_x the required number of new entrants. Here we use the technique of the service table again. A table of the following form would be calculated (for each sex, if the employment is open to both sexes).

These figures are hypothetical as is also the assumption that the entry age is twenty and that retirement takes place not later than at age sixty-five.

(For a full explanation of technique, reference might be made to 'The Length of Working Life of Males in Great Britain', a report by the Ministry of Labour, published by H.M.S.O. 1959.)

Males employed in particular occupation

Age x	l_x^w Employed	d_x^w Dying in employment	r_x^w Resigning or retiring
20	10,000	11	504
21	9,485	11	373
22	9,101	12	310
23	8,879	12	261
etc.			
64	4,562	202	4,360

If the underlying death and retirement rates had persisted for forty-five years or so, i.e. if steady state conditions could be presumed to have prevailed, then this table would represent a model of the working population in the particular occupation. If such an assumption were possible, then we have, using life table notation,

$$L_x^w = \text{number in employment at age } x \text{ last birthday}$$
$$= \tfrac{1}{2}(l_x^w + l_{x+1}^w)$$

except for L_{64}^w where since the lack of retirements occur abruptly at age 65 exact, the value to be used for l_{65}^w is $[l_{64}^w - d_{64}^w - p_{64}^{rw}]$, p_{64}^{rw} being the premature retirements before age 65. The standing population in the occupation would be

$$\sum_{20}^{64} L_x^w = \tfrac{1}{2}l_{20}^w + \sum_{21}^{64} l_x^w + \tfrac{1}{2}[l_{64}^w - d_{64}^w - p_{64}^{rw}]$$
$$= T_{20}^w$$

If the total manpower engaged in the occupation is (say) 23,500, we may write $n_{20} = 10,000 \cdot [23,500/T_{20}^w]$.

The average number of years worked in the occupation before leaving (either by resignation, retirement or death in service) is T_{20}^w/l_{20}^w.

By breaking T_{20}^w into age groups, the steady state age structure may be examined.

Steady state conditions never do exist for a sufficient length of time for the service table to be reproduced in actual experience. The first step therefore is to compare the actual age distribution (at a recent census) with that which would be characteristic of the steady state. The technique of the population pyramid is useful here (p. 15). The difference between the two distributions will indicate the degree of instability in the actual current age distribution and the likely changes that will take place before a steady state can be reached. Any special measures, e.g. to increase the intake into the particular occupation, will themselves introduce subsequent deviations from steady state conditions but these can be forecast by using the same service table technique as used above.

Career Planning

If we now turn to the consideration of a single establishment we can see that the service table technique can be used to plan intake and promotion arrangements so as to provide career opportunities that are sufficiently attractive to assist recruitment and sufficiently adapted to the needs of the establishment so as to provide a sufficient flow of personnel of the right calibre at various levels of skill or responsibility.

Let us simplify the problem and consider an establishment with three grades of staff A, B, C, grade C being the most senior. Entry into grade A occurs at age x. Grade B is maintained by promotion from grade A occurring at average age $(x + n)$ and suffers promotion out of it into grade C occurring at average age $(x + n + m)$. Retirement from all grades is at or before age sixty-five. We then have three pyramids super-imposed on each other (Figure Two). Consider Grade A between ages x and $x + n$ with an intake of l_x^A. We need to estimate l_{x+n}^A who remain in the grade at age $x + n$ and who are eligible for promotion. It is convenient to use the concept of the force of withdrawal (resignation or retirement or dismissal), i.e. the instantaneous rate of withdrawal $\overset{A}{\mu}_x$ defined as

$$- \left[\frac{d}{dx} \cdot l_x^A \right] \bigg/ l_x^A = - \frac{d}{dx} \cdot \log_e l_x^{\overset{A}{\cdot}}$$

so that

$$\log_e \cdot {}_np_x^A = \log_e l_{x+n}^A - \log_e l_x^A$$

$$= - \int_0^n \mu_{x+t}^A \cdot dt$$

$$_np_x^A = \exp \cdot \left(- \int_0^n \mu_{x+t}^A \cdot dt \right)$$

μ_x is usually derived by calculating average (central) withdrawal rates m_x at successive ages (or age groups to which a mean age can be applied) and remembering that $m_x = \mu_{x+\frac{1}{2}}$ approx.

Hence $l_{x+n}^A = l_x^A \cdot {}_np_x^A$ can be estimated.

If (say) 20 per cent are promoted at age $x + m$ to grade B we then continue to observe $0.8(l^A_{x+n})$ until age sixty-five and we commence to observe $0.2(l^A_{x+n}) = l^B_{x+n}$ subject to its own wastage rates, i.e. $l^B_{x+n+m} = l^B_{x+n} \cdot {}_m p^B_{x+n}$.

Finally if 30 per cent are promoted at age $x + n + m$ to grade C we have $0.3(l^B_{x+n+m}) = l^C_{x+n+m}$.

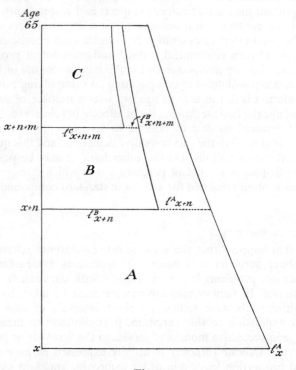

Fig.2

The total number of employees in each grade, under steady state conditions is

$$C \quad \int_0^{65-m-n-x} l^C_{x+n+m+t} \cdot \mathrm{d}t = P_C$$

$$B \quad \int_0^m l^B_{x+n+t} \cdot \mathrm{d}t = P_B$$

$$A \quad \int_0^n l^A_{x+t} \cdot \mathrm{d}t = P_A$$

If the relative numbers in the grades are fixed, e.g.

$$P_A : P_B : P_C :: 4 : 2 : 1$$

we can determine P_A and thence l_x^A. We can also calculate at any age $x + n + t$ $(t < m)$, the proportion of all surviving staff who have become promoted to grade B, i.e. $l_{x+n+t}^B / (l_{x+n+t}^B + l_{x+n+t}^A)$. This is an important measure of career prospects and is sometimes referred to as the career factor. It is usual to adjust relative numbers in grades and the promotion rates until a reasonable compromise has been achieved between economical staffing and recruitment prospects—between attracting manpower and making optimum use of it.

There are possibilities of complicating and simplifying this model. If promotion is not at a fixed age but over a number of successive years of age the basic technique is not affected but clearly each generation of promotions and of failures to secure promotion must be separately treated in the survivorship calculations and this makes the arithmetic more tedious. On the other hand it may be possible to assume that μ_x is a constant percentage δ in which case $_np_x = e^{-n\delta}$ and this is often tabulated for n and δ in standard compound interest tables.

Labour Turnover

It often happens that the wastage rate (sometimes referred to as the labour turnover rate because it represents a measure of the replacement problem) is varying rapidly with duration from entry into service. In such circumstances care must be taken to observe the withdrawals over sufficiently short intervals of time to give proper expression to this variation. It is common to measure the wastage in successive months of service in the first year or two years of service. Labour turnover is usually expressed as an equivalent annual proportion leaving in order to provide standard *dimensions* for comparison between rates for different intervals of time though it is not realistic to assume that the wastage in the first three months of service *could* persist for a whole year (it might on an annual basis be more than 100 per cent).

Useful parameters are:

Proportion of entrants at age x surviving after time w,

$$_wp_x = \exp . \left[- \int_0^w \mu_t . \, dt \right]$$

where μ_t = wastage rate in the interval t to $t + dt$.

TABLE EIGHTEEN
Labour turnover

Service duration (months)	Leavers	Mean number employed in duration interval during one year of observation	Central leaving rate (p.a.)		Proportion surviving from beginning to end of interval	Proportion surviving from entry to end of interval
			Observed	Smoothed		
0–1	205	88·5	2·321	2·40	0·818	0·818
1–2	128	74·5	1·718	1·68	0·870	0·712
2–3	79	65·0	1·215	1·30	0·897	0·638
3–6	128	153·5	0·834	0·835	0·811	0·518
6–9	33	154·5	0·343	0·390	0·906	0·469
9–12	45	164·5	0·274	0·255	0·938	0·440
(years)						
1–2	75	426·5	0·176	0·193	0·824	0·363
2–5	169	1191·0	0·142	0·121	0·693	0·252
5–10	56	784·5	0·071	0·070	0·702	0·177
10–15	61	1537·5	0·040	0·045	0·798	0·141
15–20	26	790·0	0·033	0·038	0·827	0·117
20+	61	1706·0	0·036	0·034		

Labour turnover or wastage rate for period t_1 to t_2

$$= \left[\int_{t_1}^{t_2} \mu_t \cdot dt \right] \frac{12}{t_2 - t_1}$$

if t_1 and t_2 are in months.

Expectation of service (analogous to expectation of life)

$$= \int_0^\infty t \cdot {}_t p_x \cdot \mu_{x+t} \cdot dt$$

In practice plotted values of ${}_t p_x$ are often found to follow approximately a log. normal curve. In such circumstances the calculations are simplified since tabulated values will be available for the integrals involved.

On the other hand since the number of employees involved is often comparatively small (smaller certainly than is involved in normal life table calculations) the observed leaving rates and survival proportions are likely to vary irregularly with duration. It will be necessary to graduate these values, i.e. to estimate true values that follow a smoother progression with advancing duration from entry. In such circumstances mathematical refinements will be inappropriate and considerable approximation will have to be tolerated. For this reason it will probably be preferable to proceed more directly by calculation of the service table. It is likely that such a table will in any case be more intelligible to management than a mathematical curve.

In Table Eighteen, the proportion surviving from the beginning to the end of a duration interval of t years in length has been calculated as $(2 - t \cdot m)/(2 + t \cdot m)$ where m is the central *annual* rate of withdrawal for the interval. It is also possible to assume that $t \cdot m = \int \mu$ approx. $= -\log_e {}_t p$ approx., e.g. for the first interval $t \cdot m = 0\cdot20$ and therefore the proportion surviving the first interval is

$$\log_e^{-1} [-0\cdot20] = 0\cdot818$$

and $_{20}p = \log_e^{-1} [\Sigma tm] = \log_e^{-1} - [0\cdot200 + 0\cdot140 + 0\cdot108 \ldots$
$$+ 0\cdot225 + 0\cdot190]$$

or $0\cdot118$ as compared with $0\cdot117$ in the table.

REFERENCES

Jones, E. 'Officer Career Planning (Royal Navy)', *Proceedings of the 1967 Conference of Operational Research Society* (1961).

INDEX

Antonosky, A., 106R
Barley, R. G., 141R
Benjamin, B., 15R, 73R, 106R, 141R
Birth and Death Registration Act 1953, 16
Births, correction for residence, 17
Births, projection of, 120
Bonham, D. G., 106R
Bradford Hill, A., 15R, 141R
Butler, N. R., 106R

Cancer, 129
Career structure, 152
Carrier, N. H., 111R
Census 1951, Housing Report, 6
Census organization, 47
Communicable disease, 125
Community Health Records, 138
Cox, P. R., 15R

Deaths, correction for residence, 18
Demographic Yearbook, 8
Dependency, 38

Education, 4, 47
Eugenics Review, 20R

Family analysis, 32
Fertility
  census analyses, 31
  comparability factors, 55
  factors in, 53, 65
  generation analysis, 62
  legitimacy, 56
  marriage duration, 57
  multiple births, 56
  rates, 54
  replacement, 58
Field studies, 13

General practitioner statistics, 136
General Register Office, 15R, 65R, 106R, 141R
Glass, D. V., 66R
Government Actuary, 8
Grebenik, E., 66R

Greenwood, M., 105R
Greville, T. N. E., 106R
Guide to Official Sources No. 2, 52R
Haenszel, W., 106R
Hajnal, J., 73R
Heady, J. A., 141R
Health services and population, 5
Hobson, W., 141R
Hospital statistics, 135
Household analysis, 32
Housing analysis, 36
Housing and population, 7, 32

Income, 39
Industry, 39
Industry classification, 144
Insurance sickness records, 130
International passenger survey, 109
Isaac, J., 111R

Jeffery, J. R., 111R
Jones, E., 158R

Karn, M. N., 106R
Kiser, C. V., 66R
Knowelden, J., 141R
Kohn, R., 106R

Labour turnover, 156
Liddell, F. D. K., 106R
Life tables, 10, 95
Logan, W. P. D., 106R

Manpower, 5, 142
Marriage
  factors in, 68
  nuptiality table, 69
  rates, 67
Meade, J. E., 66R
Mental disorder, 137
Migration
  internal, 45
  international, 3, 108
Milbank Memorial Quarterly, 20R
Morris, J. M., 141R

Mortality
  age and sex variation, 76
  indices, 78
  infant, 85
  life table, 95
  longitudinal studies, 103
  occupational, 88
  rates, 74
  socio-economic factors, 90
  standardization, 79
  years of life lost, 105

Newton, M. P., 111R
Normality, 123
Notification of births, 17

Occupation classification, 143

Parkes, A. S., 66R
Pemberton, J., 141R
Population
  density, 1
  estimation, 112
  index, 20R
  projection, 13, 112, 117
  pyramids, 15
  replacement, 58
  Royal Commission, 1
  studies, 20R
Population census
  districts, 48
  errors, 49
  general, 21
  organization, 47
  topics, 22
"Population" (I.N.E.D.), 20R

Population (Statistics) Act 1960, 17
Public Health Act 1936, 17

Rates, types of, 10
Registration
  births, 16
  deaths, 18
  marriages, 19

Sampling, 13
Schneider, J. R. L., 122R
Scott, J. A., 106R
Service tables, 152
Sickness measurement, 12, 123
Snow, D. J. R., 106R
Snow, E. C., 106R
Social and economic classification, 148
Socio-economic groups, 41, 149
Social security and population, 7
Social survey, 134
Standardization of rates, 79
Stocks, P., 141R
Survival factors, 103

Taylor, I., 141R
Thompson, E. J., 122R
Tuberculosis, 127

U.N. Handbook on Population Census
  Methods, 52R

Yates, F., 15R
Years of life lost, 105
Yerushalmy, J., 106R

World Population Conference 1965,
  66R, 73R, 106R

GEORGE ALLEN & UNWIN LTD
London: 40 Museum Street, W.C.1

Auckland: P.O. Box 36013, Northcote Central N.4
Barbados: P.O. Box 222, Bridgetown
Bombay: 15 Graham Road, Ballard Estate, Bombay 1
Buenos Aires: Escritorio 454–459, Florida 165
Beirut: Deeb Building, Jeanne d'Arc Street
Calcutta: 17 Chittaranjan Avenue, Calcutta 13
Cape Town: 68 Shortmarket Street
Hong Kong: 105 Wing On Mansion, 26 Hancow Road, Kowloon
Ibadan: P.O. Box 62
Karachi: Karachi Chambers, McLeod Road
Madras: Mohan Mansions, 38c Mount Road, Madras 6
Mexico: Villalongin 32, Piso, Mexico 5, D.F.
Nairobi: P.O. Box 30583
New Delhi: 13–14 Asaf Ali Road, New Delhi 1
Ontario: 81 Curlew Drive, Don Mills
Philippines: P.O. Box 4322, Manila
Rio de Janeiro: Caixa Postal 2537-Zc-00
Singapore: 36c Prinsep Street, Singapore 7
Sydney N.S.W.: Bradbury House, 55 York Street
Tokyo: P.O. Box 26, Kamata

PROFESSOR R. N. MORRIS

Urban Sociology

Sociologists have discussed many features of urban life, utilizing a variety of approaches and stressing different elements, but there is no universal agreement as to which features of the city are central and which are of minor importance. Judgements of this nature can be made only as fully fledged theories of city life are developed, tested and compared. The object of this book, therefore, is not to argue that one conception of the city is best. Professor Morris bases his discussion on a careful analysis of one theory, that of Louis Wirth, and uses this as an aid to understanding urban life, and as an introduction to the sociology of the subject.

The starting-point is Louis Wirth's classic article, 'Urbanism as a Way of Life', which aimed to present a relatively concise theory of city life which would incorporate the main research findings of the 'Chicago School' over the preceding twenty years. Professor Morris then discusses the two major approaches to the subject: the ecological, which assumes that the essence of the city lies in the concentration of a very large number of persons in a relatively small space, and the organizational, which begins with patterns of social behaviour and not the location of one's residence. While few writers have followed one approach and altogether ignored the other, their divergencies are apt to lead to confusion, partly because they have been prone to seek very simple accounts of urban life, and to look for a small number of elements from which to expect a full understanding of it.

Professor Morris concludes that the city is significant, not only because it is large and densely settled, not only because its internal organisation tends to be different from that of the countryside, but also because it influences and is influenced by groups whose members live far beyond its own boundaries. It cannot be accurately viewed as an independent social system: it is but one constituent part—often a dominant part—of a complex society.

In the author's words: 'Theory should be judged by the questions it provokes, and not merely by the answers it supplies to existing questions.' *Urban Sociology* will prove an extremely useful introduction for students who will benefit from the relative simplicity of Professor Morris' comparative approach.

LONDON: GEORGE ALLEN & UNWIN LTD